A FEAST *for the* HEART

A FEAST *for the* HEART

ENTERTAINING WITH ELEGANT AND EASY
LOW-CHOLESTEROL MENUS

Willa Gelber
with Greg Case

Helen Rothstein Kimmel, M.S., R.D.E., Nutrition Consultant

Foreword by Eliot A. Brinton, M.D.

LITTLE, BROWN AND COMPANY
Boston   Toronto   London

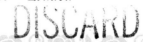

First Edition

Library of Congress Cataloging-in-Publication Data

Gelber, Willa.
    A feast for the heart: entertaining with elegant and easy
low-cholesterol menus / Willa Gelber; with Greg Case;
Helen Rothstein Kimmel, nutrition consultant; foreword by
Eliot A. Brinton.—1st ed.
        p.   cm.
    Includes index.
    ISBN 0-316-30744-0
    1. Low-cholesterol diet—Recipes.   I. Case, Greg, 1961–
II. Title.
RM 237.75.G46   1992
    641.5'638—dc20   92-3225

10   9   8   7   6   5   4   3   2   1

MV-NY

Published simultaneously in Canada
by Little, Brown & Company (Canada) Limited

Printed in the United States of America

To my husband, Karl, without whom this book
would never have gotten started, let alone finished,
and my daughter, Lucy, my heart's delight

—W. G.

Contents

A FEAST *for the* HEART

Foreword

Eliot A. Brinton, M.D.

For the past thirty years or so the American public has been swept by an ever-increasing tide of media reports about cholesterol, especially about cholesterol and fat in the diet. Cholesterol has become a household word; a majority of adult Americans have had their cholesterol levels tested, and many are actively trying to lower their levels by diet and other appropriate life-style modifications. Despite our difficulties, our occasional or frequent backsliding and cheating, most Americans do remarkably well at this task. No other country in the world has made such a dramatic voluntary improvement in diet over so short a time. Furthermore, no other country has seen such a striking decline in the frequency of heart and vascular disease. Death rates from cardiovascular disease are now nearly 50 percent lower (when adjusted for increasing average age) than thirty years ago. In striking contrast, England and most of the rest of Europe have had little or no decline in these rates over the same period of time.

While some of the credit for the improvements in cardiovascular health in this country belongs to decreased smoking and to advances in medical and surgical treatments, most of the benefit should be attributed to dietary change. Other countries that share our modern medical technology but that do not share our zeal for dietary restraint have not enjoyed the same decreases in heart and vascular disease risk. Thus, Americans are reaping the rewards of being a vanguard of sorts in the Western world with regard to healthy changes in diet and life-style. In part, we have been led by the press and by the medical establishment, but primarily this is a grass-roots movement, in which the people often lead the experts. For example, many practicing physicians admit that their patients push far harder than they do in the areas of screening and treatment of cholesterol disorders. Our collective response, although incomplete and limited in many ways, is a matter of world leadership and should be a source of national pride.

Why does the message of diet and cholesterol have such universal and enduring appeal? One would think that after so many years of wall-to-wall coverage on television and radio, in newspapers, magazines, and innumerable books, we would have reached the saturation point, yet our interest continues unabated. There are three important reasons for such unflagging attention. The first is our natural preoccupation with our own health. It is said that a simple toothache can supplant a major natural or manmade disaster as the focus of one's attention. Certainly, the presence of heart disease, or the fear of developing it, can be far more distracting than a toothache and readily can command a steadfast allegiance to remedial measures. Self-preservation is a strong instinct indeed. Second, like sex, food can be a powerful source both of pleasure and of guilt. Even in our sex-obsessed society, food is the more accessible and acceptable of the two as a source of solace and as a subject of interest. Third is our thirst for scientific breakthrough. "High tech" often provides its own reason for being, and the unfolding scientific saga of cholesterol and its control has provided continual grist for the media mill.

Beyond a few headline-grabbing naysayers, there is a remarkable consensus among nutrition experts that diet is a crucial factor in heart disease. This consensus results from a consistent and convincing body of data establishing the connection between dietary intake and diseases of the heart and vessels. Heart disease and related disorders constitute an epidemic of staggering proportions, even now claiming fifteen times more lives each year than does AIDS. Over one-quarter of the victims of heart disease die without any advance warning of their problem. Furthermore, although many risk factors are known, much of the disease occurs in so-called low-risk individuals. This means that a low-cholesterol, low-fat diet is not only helpful for people who have heart disease already, or those who seem to be at high risk, but is important for everyone.

Unfortunately, in its rush to meet deadlines and in its craving for simplicity, the lay press often short-circuits the dietary education process. "Cholesterol" is handy as a single-word summary of the problem, but its overuse has perpetuated an erroneous dietary priority. Contrary to popular belief, reducing intake of saturated fat is far more important than reducing intake of cholesterol per se. The reason is that dietary saturated fat has a far greater effect than does dietary cholesterol itself on cholesterol levels in the blood and hence, presumably, on heart disease as well. Thus, the first and foremost goal in dietary modification should be to reduce saturated fat intake. A second, related priority is to reduce total fat intake. The importance of reducing total fat in the diet stems not only from a possible relationship to heart disease, but also from probable connections with other serious diseases such as breast and colon cancer, as well as obesity, with its many adverse consequences, notably adult-onset diabetes mellitus.

Fortunately, even while some are proclaiming that Americans will not tolerate a lower fat diet, our average fat intake continues to decline. Most foods low in saturated fat are also low in cholesterol, so that reduced cholesterol intake is essentially automatic on a low saturated fat diet. Shellfish may constitute an important exception to this rule. Given their very low saturated fat content and the presence of some beneficial marine oils, however, shellfish appear to be healthful on balance, and at least should not be harmful if eaten in moderation. On the positive side of the ledger, our first priority should be to increase intake of dietary fiber and a close associate of fiber, complex carbohydrate. The high-fiber, high-carbohydrate diet has been rediscovered many times, most recently in studies of the rural Chinese, which have laid to rest a number of cherished assumptions about our need for certain levels of animal protein and calcium intake.

Given the ongoing public quest for the definitive heart-healthy diet, any book on the subject may sell and sell well. But a good writer should provide more than just another book, a rehash of old ideas with occasional tidbits of new. In the 1990s a good cholesterol and diet book should accomplish two things. First, it should help reduce rather than increase confusion among the public. The cholesterol story at best is a complicated one, but it is made more complicated by the many strident voices that hold up one narrow dietary concept or another without regard to its relationship to the whole. Second, such a book should take a positive approach, spending at least as much time talking about what we should eat as about what we should not eat. Guilt may be a great motivator in avoiding the bad, but it is always outdone in the long run by attraction to the good.

This book, I believe, performs handsomely in both respects. Not a "miracle cure" approach, it promotes variety and common sense in eating instead of excess consumption of one or more special foods. More significant, it casts current dietary recommendations in a positive light. More than any other such volume of which I am aware, it entices us to good behavior rather than browbeating us out of bad. It demonstrates that holiday cooking, party food, and gourmet meals need not be soaked in saturated fat, nor choked with cholesterol, thus carrying the aftertaste of guilt. Food can be healthful and delicious at the same time, not just on a daily basis, but even on special occasions. This is not to say that any deviation from a healthy diet carries dire consequences. Intermittent departures from the healthiest of dietary principles are not harmful as long as they remain intermittent. Nevertheless, the ultimate test of our dietary revolution is to vanquish the concept that the very best and most enjoyable cuisine is always dangerous and forbidden. The message of this book is that we do *not* have to choose between a sense of perpetual deprivation and a reckless disregard for our own mortality. The finest and most appealing food can prevent rather than promote disease. With the ideas in this book, health never needs to be sacrificed for quality, taste, and the pleasure of eating.

Eliot A. Brinton, M.D., is assistant professor and associate physician at the Laboratory of Biochemical Genetics and Metabolism, The Rockefeller University, New York, New York.

Nutritionist's Note

Helen Rothstein Kimmel, M.S., R.D.E.

Sophisticated dinner parties have traditionally been high-cholesterol, fatty affairs. When I was asked to help create a healthier entertainment cookbook, I was quite skeptical. Dozens of low-fat and low-cholesterol cookbooks claiming to contain exciting recipes are merely a disappointing array of broiled chicken dishes with fancy names. *A Feast for the Heart* proved to be a delightful surprise. Unique recipes for traditional favorites like Grand Aioli and tempting new dishes like Beet Risotto, in addition to recipes for formerly forbidden foods such as Lobster Bisque and Crème Caramel, were included. Their arrangement into seasonal, holiday, and cocktail menus eases the pressure of party planning. *A Feast for the Heart* is the perfect entertaining book for the health-conscious nineties.

FATS, CHOLESTEROL, AND YOUR DIET

The healthiest diet is not composed of rigid requirements — variety and moderation are the key! Long-term dietary changes can better be achieved by allowing a controlled amount of your favorite foods, rather than by deprivation.

Fats in food can be placed in two categories: saturated and unsaturated. Saturated fats are the "bad" fats, for they tend to raise cholesterol levels in the blood. Saturated fats are easily recognized; they are solid at room temperature and are found primarily in animal products such as meats, whole milk products, and butter. Hydrogenated vegetable shortenings and palm and coconut oils are also highly saturated. Unsaturated fat is made up of monounsaturated and polyunsaturated fatty acids. These fats may lower blood cholesterol and are therefore known as "good" fats. Certain vegetable oils such as canola oil are high in unsaturated fats.

Cholesterol is not a fat. It is a waxy substance found in all animal products. The human body produces cholesterol as well. Therefore, it is easy to obtain an excess of cholesterol from the diet, leading to plaque buildup in the arteries.

Consumption of excess fat and cholesterol has been recognized as a contributing factor in many diseases, ranging from cancer to atherosclerosis. Today, nutritionists are concerned with how many of the calories we consume come from total fat and saturated fat. To calculate the proportion of calories from fats in a food or recipe, multiply the number of grams of fat or saturated fat by 9, and compare the result to the total number of calories in the item. Ideally, we should all strive to limit the calories from fat in our diet to 30 percent of total calories. Saturated fat calories should not exceed 10 percent. Cholesterol should be limited to 300 milligrams per day.

These guidelines apply to your intake over a day or several days; every single food item or meal does not need to comply with these guidelines. The menus in *A Feast for the Heart* all derive less than 10 percent of calories from saturated fat and have less (usually far less) than 300 milligrams of cholesterol per serving. While all of the recipes have been created to be lower in fat, occasional menus derive more than 30 percent of their calories from fat. These meals, such as the Christmas dinner, still have significantly less fat than a traditional meal, and a healthy diet can be maintained if several lower fat meals are included during that week.

ABOUT THE NUTRITIONAL ANALYSIS

My role as nutritionist in the creation of *A Feast for the Heart* was to analyze the recipes and provide nutritional values for the reader. Unless otherwise stated, all recipes are created for six servings, with the analysis provided per serving. The figures given are averages and have generally been rounded off to the nearest whole number. Thus, for example, a sauce having 0.2 grams of saturated fat per serving may be described as having 0 grams saturated fat, and a sauce having 0.6 grams per serving as having 1 gram.

Several techniques have been used to lower fat and cholesterol levels in *A Feast for the Heart*. Many of the recipes were developed using canola oil, which has less saturated fat than any other commonly used cooking oil such as safflower or olive. Nonstick pans were used to reduce the amount of oil needed in a recipe. Turkey bacon was used in place of pork, and evaporated skim milk was substituted for whole milk. The use of turkey in exciting dishes like osso buco and burritos shows how fatty meats are not needed to create satisfying meals. The emphasis on exotic herbs, spices, fruits, and vegetables provides interesting taste and texture combinations.

A Feast for the Heart is a cookbook that will allow you to entertain without providing your guests with unneeded fats and cholesterol. It proves that healthier eating need not be boring.

Helen Rothstein Kimmel, M.S., R.D.E., is a nutritionist and food consultant. Currently, she is president of Foodworks, Inc., a consulting firm based in Princeton, New Jersey. She has provided nutrition consultations for Reader's Digest Creative Cooking Club, *Kosher Gourmet* magazine, and The Joseph Baum and Michael Whiteman Company.

Acknowledgments

So many people have contributed to this project:

my editor, Jennifer Josephy, who really believed in this book;

the many fine cooks whose fine recipes have enriched it;

nutritionist Helen Kimmel, whose generous effort and expertise helped make it credible;

Bob Posch, whose timely recipe writing and development were a godsend;

friends like Bonnie Bernstein, Ann Bramson, Lora and David Brody, Sylvia Carter, Laurie Colwin, Larry and Sandy Dinoff, Rozanne Gold, Nancy Jenkins, Nicholas Malgieri, George Moskowitz, Dorothy Murray, Irene Sax, Philip Schulz, and Lois Schwartz;

my parents, Ben and Ida Gelber;

and finally, and above all, my beloved friend Greg Case.

To all of you, thank you.

—W.G.

Introduction

I wish I could say that my interest in cholesterol control is purely academic. I can't. By the age of forty, I had a cholesterol count so high (391!) it threatened to prevent me from seeing my daughter grow up.

I was shocked then. It seems perfectly understandable now. I had been a gourmand from childhood, my tastes running to those very foods that are the leaders on the what-not-to-eat list of any heart-healthy diet. My breakfast order never varied: orange juice, two scrambled eggs cooked in butter, bacon on the side, and a jelly doughnut for dessert. Lunches always included anything with heavy mayonnaise in the title, until adolescence, when I switched to burgers and fries. Following after-school snacks full of saturated fats, dinner was red meat, lots of it, or chicken, often fried, with all that scrumptious skin reserved just for me. Creamy mashed potatoes came loaded with butter, along with a green vegetable sweetened with even more. In winter I drank creamy hot chocolate; in summer every evening meant ice cream. Nobody was talking about cholesterol.

I started cooking in high school, thanks to my friend Ruth Fessel, who had been raised in Europe. She was the only kid I ever knew whose mother spread cream cheese on her cold-cut sandwiches. I was impressed. I ate veal kidneys at their table and instantly fell in love. I tried them at mine and my family threatened to throw me out. I needed my own kitchen. I got it at twenty and spent my happiest moments there. I lunched on porterhouse steaks and salads bathed in blue cheese. I gave dinner parties and discovered wine and cheese (other than Velveeta, which had previously been my favorite). I put cream in everything.

In between meals I did manage to finish school and establish myself professionally, but my heart (unbeknownst to me in grave danger) remained in the kitchen. I went on to marry, bought a house, and lived for Saturday night, when I was usually preparing a multicourse feast for family and friends or indulging in one at the home of another nouveau gourmet.

Food began taking up more and more of my time. I studied it, thought about it, read about it, talked about it. Finally I went to chef's school and got a part-time job in a restaurant next to my office, working nights and weekends. Then I became a caterer. This was great. Finally I was getting paid to do the thing I most enjoyed. I had to test every prospective recipe on myself, go to all the latest restaurants as part of my research, and make at least one yearly pilgrimage to France to worship at the shrine of crème fraîche.

I was happy as a clam, or should I say an ostrich whose head would still be in the sand had my doctor not blown the whistle: my cholesterol level was almost 400. He put me on an incredibly restricted diet and gave me two months to clean up my act. If things didn't radically change, I would have to take medication for the rest of my life. He also referred me to Dr. Eliot Brinton, who was heading a research program for people like me at Rockefeller University. I was interviewed and evaluated after giving up what seemed at the time to be most of my blood.

Dr. Brinton emphasized the importance of finding a new eating style. The convert became a zealot. I began by consulting the ever-expanding collections of low-cholesterol cookbooks in bookstores and libraries. Very little help there. Recipes either didn't work, were not really low-cholesterol, or worst and most often, were almost totally devoid of flavor. I was discouraged but determined. I would just have to do it myself.

Certain favorite foods did have to be eliminated, but lots of beloved recipes could be salvaged. The challenge was invigorating. And then I noticed something interesting happening. My catering clients began asking for lighter fare. "No red meat." "My husband's watching his cholesterol." "The guest of honor has a heart condition." I was ready. The results were gratifying. My own cholesterol count dropped two hundred points, thanks to my new way of eating, and I was becoming known in the food world as a caterer with special acumen in low-cholesterol cuisine. Hostesses boasted that their heart-healthy meals delighted their guests and were so sumptuous that nobody guessed they were eating food that was good for them.

What was most amazing was that this food didn't take days to prepare, or need a Cordon Bleu diploma to execute. Friends urged me to write a cookbook for people like me who need to pay serious attention to the saturated fat and cholesterol in their diets, and for everyone else, since we all ought to eat this way.

This book, then, is for all of you. Here are the same recipes my staff and I offer our most discerning clientele. And you can make them easily in your own kitchen, often in a surprisingly short amount of time. Recipes have been developed by beloved friend and colleague Greg Case, our pastry and sous-chef, who deserves a place in culinary history if only for inventing heart-healthy brownies and cassoulet.

We have arranged the recipes by menu and season, the very same way we do as caterers, starting with fall, which is when our year begins. Each of the menus is designed to serve six, except for two at the end of the book, a special-occasion buffet for twelve, and a cocktail party with hors d'oeuvres for twenty-five. But all recipes are easy to multiply or divide, depending on who's eating, so you can use them to feed your family as well as your friends.

Be flexible in working with these menus. Fresh food is at its peak in its season, but today, with the world as our marketplace, there's no reason a winter favorite can't be savored in spring. Don't reject the idea of buying a starter or dessert if it makes life easier. And please, leave out a course if it's too much (food or work). Or add one of your own.

We suggest that you pay close attention to the introductions that precede each recipe for suggestions about serving, substitutions, and other ways these recipes can be used. The final chapter on stocks and sauces perhaps should have come first, since it is so important to have these staples on hand as the foundation of a number of the recipes. Get in the habit of making them when you're not entertaining, to make life easier when you are. Remember, successful entertaining depends on a relaxed host.

To your health, and eat hearty!

—W.G.

FALL

Bountiful Breakfast Buffet

Serves 6

Mimosas

Blueberry Soup

Cornmeal Cakes

Whipped Yogurt Cream

Maple-Walnut Sauce

Brandied Peach Sauce

Chicken Sausage Patties

Orange Marmalade Muffins

Banana-Pecan Muffins

Mimosas

This festive morning beverage is always a party favorite. Serve it as a reception cocktail as your guests arrive, and offer refills throughout the meal. A fine champagne is always good, but a less expensive sparkling wine (a blanc de blancs or Spanish bubbly) also works well. What can't be substituted is freshly squeezed orange juice. Squeeze the oranges yourself, or buy the juice ready made at your local greengrocer. Cheers!

    1 bottle champagne, chilled
    1 pint freshly squeezed orange juice, chilled
    6 large strawberries

For each cocktail: Pour 4 ounces champagne into a tall flute glass. Pour in 2 ounces orange juice, leaving a little space at the top of each glass.
    Garnish each Mimosa with a strawberry.

1 cocktail
Cholesterol: 0 mg   Total Fat: 0 gm
Saturated Fat: 0 gm   Calories: 107

Blueberry Soup

I can never get enough blueberries. Since I'm always looking for new ways to serve them, I thought they might work as a fruit soup. I was right! Guests love this do-ahead starter, especially since the flavor of blueberries comes as a wonderful surprise in liquid form. The color, of violets, is sensational, so be sure to serve the soup in bowls that show it off.

    3 pints fresh blueberries, washed and hulled (6 cups frozen blueberries
        may be substituted)
    5 tablespoons freshly squeezed lemon juice, strained
    2¼ cups low-fat buttermilk
    6 tablespoons granulated sugar
    ¼ teaspoon salt (optional)

In the workbowl of a food processor, puree the blueberries in small batches until they are liquefied. Pass through a fine sieve to remove skin and seeds.

Combine the puree with the remaining ingredients and stir until mixture is uniformly blended.

Refrigerate until ready to serve.

Note: Soup may be refrigerated, tightly covered, up to 3 days.

Cholesterol: 3 mg   Total Fat: 2 gm
Saturated Fat: 1 gm   Calories: 175

Cornmeal Cakes

Quick! How do you make pancakes? If milk, butter, and eggs jump to mind, you know your flapjacks. And you also know you can't have them if you're watching your cholesterol, or anyone else's. We've come up with a delicious recipe that puts pancakes back on your plate. The addition of some cornmeal gives them a bit of crunch, and the buttermilk adds an interesting tang.

For best results, cook these pancakes just before you start to eat and keep them on a tray in a low oven (250 degrees) until ready to serve. Or, if you really want to show off, make them right in front of your guests on a portable griddle. Serve them up with Whipped Yogurt Cream (see page 240) and the maple-walnut and peach sauces (see following recipes) and hope that there's one left for the cook.

   3/4 cup yellow cornmeal
   3/4 cup all-purpose flour
   1/2 teaspoon baking soda
   1 teaspoon baking powder
   1/2 teaspoon salt
   2 tablespoons granulated sugar
   1 cup low-fat buttermilk
   3/4 cup water
   Grapeseed (or other vegetable) oil for frying

In a large bowl, combine cornmeal, flour, baking soda, baking powder, salt, and sugar. Stir with a whisk until well combined.

Make a well in the center of the mixture and add buttermilk and water. Stir until batter is smooth. Set aside.

In a nonstick frying pan, heat a few drops of oil (about $\frac{1}{2}$ teaspoon per pancake) over medium flame. Pour batter into pan, about 3 tablespoons per pancake, keeping the thickness approximately $\frac{1}{8}$ inch. Cook until batter bubbles in the center and outer edges are brown, 2–3 minutes. Flip and continue to cook 2–3 minutes more, or until browned. Remove and keep warm.

Continue with remaining batter, adding a small amount of oil to the frying pan before cooking each batch.

Yield: About 18 small (3–3$\frac{1}{2}$-inch) pancakes

1 pancake
Cholesterol: 1 mg   Total Fat: 2 gm
Saturated Fat: 0 gm   Calories: 68

Maple-Walnut Sauce

For the serious maple syrup lovers among you, I've recently been told that it's possible to lease your own maple tree in Vermont and receive all the ambrosial syrup that it produces. This service is said to come complete with regular written communiqués direct from the tree. But pure maple syrup is even available at your local supermarket. And with only three other ingredients and 20 minutes, you'll have a fabulous sauce for pancakes.

$\frac{1}{2}$ cup toasted walnuts, finely ground
2 cups pure maple syrup
$\frac{1}{4}$ cup freshly squeezed orange juice, strained
1 cinnamon stick

Combine all ingredients in a saucepan and simmer over medium flame, stirring occasionally, for approximately 10 minutes.

Remove cinnamon stick before serving.

Yield: 2¹/₂ cups
Note: Sauce may be refrigerated, tightly covered, up to 2 weeks.

2 tablespoons
Cholesterol: 0 mg   Total Fat: 1 gm
Saturated Fat: 0 gm   Calories: 112

Brandied Peach Sauce

Although this sauce takes only minutes to make, it will do you proud. The secret is to use only the best and freshest ingredients. When selecting the fruit, close your eyes and sniff. You should be able to inhale the essence of peach. Use a good brandy. People wrongly assume that quality is unimportant if alcohol is to be cooked. And check your ginger jar. If it has been sitting on the spice shelf since you learned to cook, the ginger needs replacing.

This sauce also works wonderfully as a dessert topping, but you may not have any leftovers to use this way unless you make extra!

4 large ripe peaches, pits removed and fruit quartered
¹/₄ cup granulated sugar
2 tablespoons brandy
¹/₂ teaspoon ground ginger

In the workbowl of a food processor, puree all ingredients. Pass through a sieve to remove peach skins. Refrigerate sauce until ready to serve.

Yield: 2 cups
Note: Sauce may be refrigerated, tightly covered, up to a week.

2 tablespoons
Cholesterol: 0 mg   Total Fat: 0 gm
Saturated Fat: 0 gm   Calories: 24

Chicken Sausage Patties

There is something about a pancake that cries out for a sausage. There is everything about a sausage that makes it a cholesterol no-no; everything except the spices that give it its unique flavor. To find an acceptable alternative, we eliminated all the bad stuff and started with the seasoning. It took some doing, but we finally came up with a breakfast sausage worthy of its name.

1 pound chicken breasts, skinned, boned, and cut into 1-inch pieces
1 small garlic clove, peeled and coarsely chopped (about 1 teaspoon)
$\frac{1}{4}$ cup chopped fresh parsley
$\frac{1}{4}$ teaspoon ground thyme
$\frac{1}{8}$ teaspoon ground sage
$\frac{1}{8}$ teaspoon cayenne pepper
$\frac{1}{2}$ teaspoon freshly ground black pepper
1 teaspoon salt
2 large egg whites
3 tablespoons canola (or other vegetable) oil
Bread crumbs for coating patties
Vegetable oil for frying

In the workbowl of a food processor combine chicken breasts, garlic, parsley, spices, egg whites, and oil. Using short pulses, process until smooth, 2–3 minutes.

Remove mixture from bowl and portion evenly into 12 balls. Roll each ball in bread crumbs. Press into thin, flat patties about $\frac{1}{4}$ inch thick.

Place patties on a baking sheet lined with plastic wrap and refrigerate at least 15 minutes, and up to 24 hours, before cooking. Remove patties from refrigerator and redredge in bread crumbs before frying.

To cook, heat a few drops of oil in a nonstick frying pan over medium-high flame. Brown patties on both sides, 3–4 minutes per side.

Yield: 12 patties

Note: These taste best with last-minute cooking, so do them up just before you sit down to eat and keep them warm in a low oven until you're ready for them.

1 patty
Cholesterol: 23 mg   Total Fat: 6 gm
Saturated Fat: 1 gm   Calories: 119

Orange Marmalade Muffins

What makes this brunch so successful is the options. A surprising number of guests go the distance and eat everything. Some fill up on a couple of helpings of Blueberry Soup. And there are always a couple who stop at a muffin and coffee. We feel for these people, so we make our muffins memorable. The secret ingredient in these is orange marmalade, which adds an intense orange flavor. The crunch topping contributes textural interest. With all the good things contained within, this is a meal in a muffin.

2 cups oat bran
1/2 cup cake flour
1/2 teaspoon baking soda
1 tablespoon baking powder
1/2 teaspoon salt
2 large egg whites
3 tablespoons canola (or other vegetable) oil
2/3 cup skim milk
1/3 cup freshly squeezed orange juice, strained
1 cup orange marmalade
Zest of 2 medium oranges, finely grated

For the topping:
3/4 cup oatmeal
1/4 cup orange marmalade

Preheat oven to 425 degrees.
Line a 12-cup muffin tin with paper cups. Set aside.
In a large bowl, combine oat bran, cake flour, baking soda, baking powder, and salt. Stir with a whisk until well blended.

In a separate bowl, lightly whisk egg whites. Stir in oil, milk, orange juice, 1 cup marmalade, and orange zest.

Make a well in the center of the dry ingredients. Pour liquid mixture into well, stirring with a whisk until all the ingredients are well incorporated. Set aside.

To make topping, combine oatmeal and marmalade in a small bowl. Working with a fork, toss the mixture until all the oatmeal flakes are coated with marmalade.

Fill the muffin cups evenly with batter. Spoon topping evenly over center of muffins. Bake on middle rack of oven for 20–25 minutes, or until a toothpick inserted into the center of a muffin comes out clean. Cool on a wire rack.

Yield: 12 muffins

Note: The muffins are best when freshly baked, but they may be frozen for several weeks and reheated before serving.

1 muffin
Cholesterol: 0 mg   Total Fat: 3 gm
Saturated Fat: 0 gm   Calories: 156

Banana-Pecan Muffins

Remember banana bread? It came into my life in the sixties, along with bare feet, Bob Dylan, and Woodstock. This was the extent of my bread baking, a pastime I realized was politically correct but never found that interesting. Today people still like the comforting flavor of bananas and nuts in these muffins made without butter, whole milk, or eggs. Served warm, they are always a hit.

2 cups oat bran
1 cup cake flour
1/2 cup light brown sugar
1/2 teaspoon baking soda
1 tablespoon baking powder
1/2 teaspoon salt
1/2 teaspoon ground cinnamon
2 large egg whites

2 tablespoons canola (or other vegetable) oil
1 cup skim milk
1 teaspoon pure vanilla extract
2 cups banana pulp (3–4 overripe bananas, mashed)
1 cup pecans, coarsely chopped

Preheat oven to 425 degrees.

Line a 12-cup muffin tin with paper cups. Set aside.

In a large bowl, combine oat bran, cake flour, sugar, baking soda, baking powder, salt, and cinnamon. Stir with a whisk until well blended. Set aside.

In a separate bowl, lightly whisk egg whites. Stir in oil, milk, vanilla extract, and banana pulp.

Make a well in the center of the dry ingredients. Pour liquid mixture into well and stir with a whisk until all ingredients are well incorporated. Stir in half the pecans.

Evenly fill the muffin cups with the batter. Sprinkle remaining pecans over the tops. Bake on the middle rack of the oven for 20–25 minutes, or until a toothpick inserted into the center of a muffin comes out clean. Cool on a wire rack.

Yield: 12 muffins

Note: The muffins are best when freshly baked, but they may be frozen for several weeks and reheated before serving.

1 muffin
Cholesterol: 0 mg   Total Fat: 9 gm
Saturated Fat: 1 gm   Calories: 181

A Chili Autumn Lunch

Serves 6

Roasted Tortilla Chips
Fresh Tomato Salsa
Best Bean Chili
Sour "Cream"
Orange, Romaine, and Watercress Salad
Cornbread
Broiled Pineapple Rings
Pignoli Macaroons

Roasted Tortilla Chips

Who doesn't love chips? But anyone who's watching his diet shouldn't eat them. So we've created a chip that everyone can enjoy. Since it's oven-roasted instead of fried, there's no added fat. Set a bowl of them out with some of the salsa so guests can munch while you're finishing up in the kitchen. Then move them to the table where folks can use them as a chili garnish. Bet you can't eat just one.

One 10-ounce package soft corn tortillas

Preheat broiler.

Cut tortillas in half. Cut each half into three equal triangles. Place a single layer of the tortilla triangles on a broiler pan and broil 8–10 inches from the flame. When the pieces are golden brown, about 2 minutes, turn triangles and repeat on the other side.

Remove chips to a bowl and allow to cool. Continue cooking the remaining tortilla triangles in the same manner until all the chips have been roasted.

Note: Once cooled, the chips can be stored in an airtight container for several hours before serving.

1¹/₂ ounces chips
Cholesterol: 0 mg   Total Fat: 2 gm
Saturated Fat: 0 gm   Calories: 107

Fresh Tomato Salsa

Any cook worth her sauce has her salsa — a raw amalgam of vegetables, low in fat and high in heat. This zippy condiment is endlessly versatile. It works wonders with drinks. Just offer it with our chips, for a healthy alternative to cheese and crackers. Serve it on a piece of grilled chicken or fish for an instant entrée. Or use it as a replacement for the usual high-fat spreads on your sandwiches. And, of course, don't forget it with your chili, for a welcome taste of freshness and fire.

6 large tomatoes (very ripe)
3 scallions, bearded and thinly sliced
1 small garlic clove, peeled and minced
1 small jalapeño pepper, seeded and finely chopped
3 tablespoons coarsely chopped fresh coriander (cilantro)
1/4 teaspoon granulated sugar
Salt to taste

Wash tomatoes and pat dry. Core and finely dice. Place in a bowl along with the juice that has been released during dicing.

Add remaining ingredients and mash together with the back of a wooden spoon until a thick, soupy consistency is achieved. Taste for salt.

Cover and refrigerate at least 1 hour and no longer than 8 hours before serving.

Yield: About 6 cups

1/2 cup
Cholesterol: 0 mg   Total Fat: 0 gm
Saturated Fat: 0 gm   Calories: 21

Best Bean Chili

In my line of work I meet a lot of famous chefs. Sometimes I invite them home for dinner. I used to lose sleep obsessing about the menu. No longer. You want to know my secret? I serve chili. Everybody loves it. And this vegetarian one has the texture of meat without the cholesterol. We use pintos and red kidneys, but don't be afraid to substitute other beans. Let your guests add their own toppings. Provide as many as you can think of — chopped onions, scallions, fresh coriander, jalapeño peppers, bell peppers, tomatoes, our Sour "Cream" (see next recipe) — and watch them go wild.

1/2 pound dried pinto beans
1/2 pound dried red kidney beans
1 small onion, peeled, stuck with 2 cloves
6 cups water

¼ cup canola (or other vegetable) oil

10 ounces mushrooms, finely chopped

4–5 large garlic cloves, peeled and minced (about 2 tablespoons)

3 large onions (about 1 pound), peeled and diced

1 cup dry red wine

2 teaspoons ground cumin

1½ teaspoons dried oregano

2 bay leaves

½ teaspoon dried crushed red pepper flakes *or* 1 small jalapeño pepper,
   seeded and finely chopped (more pepper may be used for spicier chili)

1 teaspoon salt

½ teaspoon freshly ground black pepper

One 28-ounce can imported crushed plum tomatoes

2½ cups Chicken Stock (see page 235)

1 tablespoon chopped fresh coriander (cilantro)

Place pinto and kidney beans in a large stockpot. Add the onion stuck with cloves. Cover with 6 cups cold water. Bring to a boil over medium-high heat and cook 3–4 minutes.

Cover pot. Turn off heat and allow to stand 1 hour. Drain beans and set them aside. Discard liquid and clove-studded onion.

In another large pot, heat oil over medium flame until it just begins to smoke. Add mushrooms and sauté until browned, about 5 minutes, stirring occasionally. Mix in garlic and cook 1–2 minutes longer. Add onions and sauté until they are translucent, about 10 minutes.

Pour in wine and simmer 3–4 minutes. Stir in spices, tomatoes, Chicken Stock, and beans. Bring to a boil. Reduce heat and simmer uncovered, stirring occasionally, until almost all the liquid is absorbed, about 1½ hours. When the chili begins to look dry, cover pot and continue to simmer until the beans are very tender, about 2 hours more. Remove lid and stir occasionally. (If mixture becomes too dry, add a small amount of water, wine, or Chicken Stock.)

Stir in fresh coriander just before serving.

Note: The chili may be stored in the refrigerator for 6–7 days. It may also be frozen for several months. When reheating chili, add a bit of liquid to help return it to its original consistency.

Cholesterol: 0 mg   Total Fat: 12 gm
Saturated Fat: 1 gm   Calories: 341

Sour "Cream"

8 ounces 1 percent-fat cottage cheese

½ cup plain low-fat yogurt

2 teaspoons freshly squeezed lemon juice, strained

1 tablespoon granulated sugar

Place cottage cheese in the workbowl of a food processor. Using short pulses, process until smooth, 2–3 minutes.

In a separate bowl, combine cottage cheese with remaining ingredients. Stir with a whisk until homogenous.

Refrigerate at least 1 hour before serving.

Yield: 1½ cups

Note: Sour "Cream" can be refrigerated up to 6 days.

1 tablespoon
Cholesterol: 0 mg   Total Fat: 0.3 gm
Saturated Fat: 0 gm   Calories: 12

Orange, Romaine, and Watercress Salad

I've been serving this salad for twenty years. I originally found it in James Beard's *Menus for Entertaining*, and it has undergone a number of subtle changes over time. The taste of citrus cools the palate after a spicy dish like chili, and the oranges make a beautiful picture on the plate. The salad may also be used as the basis for a tasty lunch with chunks of grilled chicken or monkfish.

3 large navel oranges

1 medium red onion, peeled

4 tablespoons Orange Vinaigrette (see below)

2 medium heads romaine lettuce, trimmed of damaged leaves, washed, and
    thoroughly dried

1 large bunch watercress, stemmed, washed, and thoroughly dried
Salt
Freshly ground black pepper

Using a sharp paring knife, remove peel and white pith from each orange. Cutting between the white membranes, remove whole orange sections and reserve in a bowl. (Any juice from the fruit may be used in preparing the Orange Vinaigrette.)

Using a mandoline or very sharp knife, cut the onion as thinly as possible into rounds. Combine with orange sections and toss with the Orange Vinaigrette. Set aside.

Tear the lettuce into bite-size pieces and mix in a large salad bowl with the watercress.

Gently tossing, pour the Orange Vinaigrette and orange sections over the greens to lightly coat. Season with salt and pepper.

Note: Greens may be washed and refrigerated for several hours. Oranges and onions may be marinated and stored in the refrigerator for 2–3 hours.

Cholesterol: 0 mg   Total Fat: 3 gm
Saturated Fat: 0 gm   Calories: 90

ORANGE VINAIGRETTE

2 tablespoons balsamic vinegar
1½ teaspoons orange zest, finely grated
6 tablespoons freshly squeezed orange juice, strained
4 tablespoons canola (or other vegetable) oil
Salt
Freshly ground black pepper

In a small bowl, combine balsamic vinegar, orange zest, and orange juice. Stir with a whisk until well blended. Add the canola oil in a slow, thin stream while whisking continuously. Season with salt and pepper.

Yield: ½ cup

1 tablespoon
Cholesterol: 0 mg   Total Fat: 5 gm
Saturated Fat: 0 gm   Calories: 51

Cornbread

A slice of golden yellow cornbread is a wonderful companion to a bowl of fiery red. Its sweetness offsets the spiciness of the chili; its softness, the bite of the beans. It's also fine as a stuffing base, or toasted with jam alongside your morning coffee.

Solid vegetable shortening and flour to line pan
½ cup all-purpose flour
1½ cups yellow cornmeal
3 tablespoons granulated sugar
1 teaspoon baking powder
1 teaspoon baking soda
½ teaspoon salt
One 8-ounce can cream-style corn
2 egg whites
1½ cups buttermilk
2 tablespoons canola (or other vegetable) oil

Preheat oven to 375 degrees.

Grease a 9-inch-square baking pan with vegetable shortening and dust with flour. Invert pan and tap bottom to eliminate any excess flour. Set aside.

In a large bowl sift together ½ cup flour, cornmeal, sugar, baking powder, baking soda, and salt. Set aside.

In a separate bowl combine corn, egg whites, buttermilk, and vegetable oil. Make a well in the center of the dry ingredients and pour in the liquid ingredients. Stir just until combined.

Pour batter into the prepared baking pan. Place in the center of the oven and bake until a toothpick inserted into the middle of the cornbread comes out clean, 30–35 minutes.

Cholesterol: 52 mg　　Total Fat: 6 gm
Saturated Fat: 1 gm　　Calories: 286

Broiled Pineapple Rings

This dish was a personal favorite long before I knew about cholesterol. It is the creation of the late Felipe Rojas-Lombardi, who was chef and owner of The Ballroom restaurant in New York City. What could be simpler or better? It takes just a few minutes to make but is as enjoyable as the most elaborate dessert. Its cinnamony sugariness makes for a wonderful finale to a chili meal, but this is also a fine first course for a breakfast.

1 teaspoon ground cinnamon
$^3/_4$ cup dark brown sugar
2 small ripe pineapples, top, bottom, and skin removed; set aside one of
    the pineapple tops, with leaves attached, for garnish

Combine cinnamon and brown sugar in a small bowl. Mix until well blended. Set aside.

Preheat broiler.

Cut each pineapple into 6 equal rounds. Using a small, round cookie cutter, remove the core from each piece. Discard the core.

Place the pineapple rings on a foil-lined broiler pan. Place the pan 6–8 inches from the flame and broil fruit for 2 minutes. Remove pan from broiler and flip over each pineapple ring. Sprinkle each one with about 1 tablespoon of the cinnamon-sugar mixture.

Return pan to broiler and continue to broil until the sugar mixture begins to bubble, 2–3 minutes. Remove from broiler.

Place the reserved pineapple top, together with its leaves, on a serving tray. Surround with the pineapple rings. Serve hot.

Cholesterol: 0 mg   Total Fat: 0 gm
Saturated Fat: 0 gm   Calories: 142

Pignoli Macaroons

We thought a cookie with a subtle crunch would be nice alongside the softened, warm pineapple. We weren't wrong. This one, with its distinctive pine nut flavor, is just right. Be careful about the nuts, which are also known as pignoli. They quickly become rancid, so make sure you are buying a fresh batch, and store them in the freezer.

$1/4$ cup granulated sugar
1 tablespoon cornstarch
$1/8$ teaspoon ground allspice
$1/4$ teaspoon ground cinnamon
2 egg whites, at room temperature
$1/2$ teaspoon pure vanilla extract
$1/4$ cup pine nuts

Preheat oven to 300 degrees.

Sift together 2 tablespoons sugar, cornstarch, allspice, and cinnamon and set aside.

With a whisk or electric mixer, beat egg whites until soft peaks begin to form. Sprinkle in remaining 2 tablespoons sugar and beat until stiff peaks form. Add vanilla extract and stir just to combine.

Resift the dry ingredients over the top of the beaten egg whites. Sprinkle pine nuts over mixture and gently fold together until evenly incorporated.

Line a cookie sheet with parchment paper or a brown paper bag. Using a spoon or a pastry bag fitted with large plain tip, make small mounds of batter (about 1 inch in diameter) spaced 1 inch apart. Place in center of oven and bake until golden, about 15 minutes. Turn off oven and allow cookies to cool in oven for 1 hour. Remove from oven and allow to cool to room temperature.

Yield: 24 cookies

Note: These cookies will absorb moisture quickly and become soft. To keep them crisp, store in an airtight container at room temperature. They will keep 2–3 days.

1 cookie
Cholesterol: 0 mg   Total Fat: 2 gm
Saturated Fat: 1 gm   Calories: 34

A Spanish Supper

Serves 6

Sylvia's Sangria

Sassy Squid Salad

Rio Mar Chicken

Roasted Pepper Salad

Shoestring Fries

Crème Caramel

Sylvia's Sangria

Friend and food writer Sylvia Carter refers to this beautiful brew as an "alco-holic lemonade." A cinch to put together, it has a cool, clean taste that is a nice change from the regular red sangria we've been drinking for years. Should you miss the old sweetness, add some sugar. And if you like the look of a floating fruit salad, cut up a few of your favorites — apples, oranges, peaches — and pop them in.

    Freshly squeezed juice of 2 large lemons
    Freshly squeezed juice of 2 medium limes
    2 tablespoons Grand Marnier
    ½ cup lemon vodka (plain vodka may be substituted)
    1 liter white wine, chilled
    1 liter plain seltzer, chilled
    2 large lemons, thinly sliced, seeds removed
    2 medium limes, thinly sliced, seeds removed

Combine lemon juice, lime juice, Grand Marnier, and vodka. Chill. Just before serving, combine juice mixture with wine and seltzer. Serve in a pitcher to which the lemon and lime slices have been added.
Yield: About 2½ quarts

6 ounces
Cholesterol: 0 mg   Total Fat: 0 gm
Saturated Fat: 0 gm   Calories: 55

Sassy Squid Salad

This simple and savory seafood salad was inspired by a similar one made of octopus, served in a superb little Spanish restaurant in downtown New York City called Rio Mar. My family was introduced to this place by a Spanish friend long before it became fashionable, and for years we celebrated all important occasions there. In fact, my two-week-old daughter's first foray into the wider world was spent at their bar, cozy in the Snugli on my chest while I savored a glass of their delicious sangria.

Made with mostly simple ingredients, this first-course salad maintains a clear richness of flavor that allows each element to shine.

For the dressing:

3 tablespoons freshly squeezed lime juice
2 teaspoons very finely chopped fresh oregano
1 small garlic clove, peeled and juiced through a garlic press
1/2 teaspoon salt
1/4 teaspoon freshly ground black pepper
1/8 teaspoon ground cumin
1/2 teaspoon paprika
2 teaspoons chili oil (available in Oriental food shops)
4 tablespoons extra-virgin olive oil
1/4 pound red onion, peeled and cut into very thin rings

For the court bouillon:

2 cups water
1/2 cup dry vermouth
1/4 cup balsamic vinegar
1 small bay leaf
1 teaspoon paprika
1/4 teaspoon ground cloves
1/4 teaspoon freshly ground black pepper

The squid:

1 1/2 pounds cleaned fresh squid (tentacles and body sac), head end cut into clusters of 2 or 3 tentacles, body sac sliced crosswise into 1/4-inch rings

To complete the salad:

2 cups 1/2-inch bread cubes from cholesterol-free peasant-style bread, toasted
2 tablespoons finely chopped parsley
1/2 pound red tomatoes, quartered (optional)
1/2 pound yellow tomatoes, quartered (optional)

Make the dressing in a bowl large enough to hold the completed salad. Combine the lime juice, oregano, garlic juice, salt, pepper, cumin, paprika, and chili oil and stir with a whisk until well blended. Add the olive oil in a slow, thin stream while continuously whisking. When the oil is incorporated, stir in the red onion. Reserve.

In a pot large enough to hold all of the squid and the ingredients of the court bouillon, combine the water, vermouth, vinegar, bay leaf, paprika, cloves, and pepper. Over high heat, bring to a boil. Reduce heat and simmer, covered, for 5 minutes. Add the squid. Adjust heat to simmer. Cook for 1 additional minute, covered. Drain. Discard bay leaf.

Add drained squid to the dressing and onions. Stir. Allow to cool to room temperature. Cover and store refrigerated for 24 hours.

Immediately before serving, combine the squid with the bread cubes and parsley. Toss briefly and spoon onto 6 chilled salad plates. As an option, you may wish to garnish the salad with wedges of ripe red or yellow tomato.

Cholesterol: 55 mg   Total Fat: 11 gm
Saturated Fat: 2 gm   Calories: 236

Rio Mar Chicken

Another chorus in our lovesong to Rio Mar is our treatment of my favorite dish on their menu — Chicken Rio Mar. The chef and owner, David Romero, generously shared his recipe with me, cautioning that many have tried but none have succeeded in duplicating his dish. We were amazed to learn that a few everyday ingredients could produce such a stellar result. We used the same ones, but took the skin off the chicken to lower the fat, and stuck with dark meat, since it's juicier. We're not sure if we should tell him, but we think he would grudgingly admire our rendition.

For ease of serving, plate the chicken in the kitchen along with some of the Roasted Pepper Salad and a generous helping of Shoestring Fries (see following recipes).

6 chicken legs, separated into drumstick and thigh pieces
Salt
Freshly ground black pepper
¼ cup yellow prepared mustard
2 tablespoons Worcestershire sauce
2 tablespoons white wine

Remove skin from chicken pieces and discard. Sprinkle chicken with salt and pepper. Set aside.

In a large bowl, combine mustard, Worcestershire sauce, and wine. Add chicken pieces and turn to coat evenly. Allow to marinate 20–30 minutes.

Preheat broiler. Place chicken on broiler tray and position 8–10 inches from the flame. Cook, turning chicken pieces every 4–5 minutes, until chicken is dark and cooked through, 12–15 minutes in all.

Cholesterol: 161 mg   Total Fat: 9 gm
Saturated Fat: 2 gm   Calories: 265

Roasted Pepper Salad

I was never a courageous cook. I had an extensive cookbook collection and subscribed to all the food magazines, but when a recipe called for an involved technique, I turned the page. On account of this cowardice, for years I missed the pleasure of roasting a pepper. Don't make the same mistake! The wonderful smoky aroma alone is worth the effort. Besides, as I finally learned, there's nothing to it.

5 medium sweet red peppers
4 medium sweet green peppers
3 tablespoons extra-virgin olive oil
1 large clove garlic, peeled and minced
2 tablespoons balsamic vinegar
Salt
Freshly ground black pepper

Peppers can be roasted whole, either directly on top of a gas burner over high flame or in the broiler section of an oven. As the skin chars black, turn the peppers to blacken evenly on all sides. Remove peppers from flame or broiler and hold under cool running water, placing a colander in the sink to catch the burnt skin. Using your fingers, rub off the charred pepper skin. Remove and discard stems and seeds, and set peppers aside to drain. Cut into 1-inch strips.

In a large nonstick frying pan, heat the oil and garlic until the garlic just begins to turn golden, 3–4 minutes. Add the pepper strips. Cook until they are quite soft, 8–10 minutes. Stir in vinegar, salt, and pepper. Cook 2 minutes longer.

Remove contents of pan to a bowl. Allow to cool to room temperature before serving.

Note: This salad may be made a day in advance and kept in the refrigerator, tightly covered. However, it should be brought to room temperature before serving.

Cholesterol: 0 mg   Total Fat: 7 gm
Saturated Fat: 1 gm   Calories: 85

Shoestring Fries

So I lied. Chicken Rio Mar *is* my favorite dish at this beloved haunt — if we're talking entrées. But my conscience has been bothering me. If I had to choose my last meal on earth, it might have to be the french fries that are served to accompany this savory winner. And if I know what's good for me, I won't have them again until then. Deep-fried in a combination of soy and olive oil, they must remain the stuff that dreams are made of. Not so ours. These Shoestring Fries are baked in the oven, with relatively little oil, so you can feast on them with a clear conscience.

¹/₄ cup extra-virgin olive oil
6 medium russet potatoes (about 1¹/₂ pounds), cut into thin julienne (¹/₈ inch thick)
Salt

Preheat oven to 500 degrees.

Pour oil onto a large nonstick sheet pan (about 18 x 14 inches). Add potatoes and toss to coat with oil. Sprinkle with salt to taste. Place tray on top rack of oven and cook 7 minutes. Remove tray from oven and turn potatoes to brown evenly. Return to oven. Cook until golden brown, about 7 minutes more.

Serve immediately.

Cholesterol: 0 mg   Total Fat: 9 gm
Saturated Fat: 1 gm   Calories: 185

Crème Caramel

Authentically speaking, the correct ending to this meal would be the classic Spanish flan — a baked custard that glazes and sauces itself with the caramel that forms in its mold. But since custard means eggs, we would never have considered it if not for our friend Rozanne Gold. As food consultant to New York's enchanting Rainbow Room, she had created a crème caramel (France's version of flan) for their spa restaurant and offered to share the recipe with us. We eliminated the egg her creation called for and added evaporated skim milk, a wonderful product that is rich, sweet, and flavorful. This cholesterol-correct custard is sure to win your heart.

1 1/2 cups granulated sugar

2 cups skim milk

2 cups evaporated skim milk

2 tablespoons dark brown sugar

2 extra-large egg whites

1 teaspoon pure vanilla extract

Preheat oven to 350 degrees.

In a large saucepan melt 1 cup granulated sugar over high heat until dark amber in color, 7–8 minutes. Stir occasionally to evenly caramelize the sugar. Pour melted sugar evenly into six 7-ounce ovenproof ramekins. (Immediately rinse saucepan in very hot water to clean.) Set aside.

Pour skim milk and evaporated skim milk into a medium saucepan and scald over high heat.

Meanwhile, combine the remaining ½ cup granulated sugar, brown sugar, and egg whites in a large bowl. Stir briefly to combine. (Overbeating will cause unwanted air bubbles.) Add scalded milk slowly to sugar mixture while stirring constantly. Stir in vanilla extract.

Place ramekins in a shallow baking pan. (It must be deeper than the ramekins.) Divide the custard mixture evenly among the 6 ramekins, leaving ¼ inch free at the top of each one. Pour very hot water into the baking pan to about half the depth of the ramekins.

Loosely cover the baking pan with aluminum foil and place in the oven. Bake 50–55 minutes, or until the tip of a sharp knife inserted into the center of a custard comes out clean. Remove pan from oven and ramekins from hot water. Allow them to cool to room temperature.

Refrigerate at least 3 hours before serving. To serve, tap sides of each ramekin while inverting onto a dessert plate. Tap bottom until custard is released. Allow liquid caramel to pool around the custard.

Cholesterol: less than 1 mg	Total Fat: 0 gm
Saturated Fat: 0 gm	Calories: 302

Curry and Company

Serves 6

Red Lentil Samosas

Mango Chutney

Eggplant Pickle

Shrimp and Potato Curry

Mint and Coriander Raita

Carrot-Cucumber Sambal

Spiced Pita Bread

Tropical Fruit Salad with Candied Ginger

Red Lentil Samosas

A samosa is a savory, filled Indian pastry in the shape of a triangle. The dough is made with a clarified butter known as ghee. Traditionally, it is stuffed with meat, vegetables, or a combination of both and deep-fried. Our version uses phyllo dough, a convenient product that is easy to use, and free of fat. And we cook our samosas in the oven, rather than in an oil bath. Though an excellent hors d'oeuvre all by themselves, these samosas become an exotic first course when paired with our Mango Chutney and Eggplant Pickle — two contrasting condiments (see following recipes).

2 teaspoons canola (or other vegetable) oil
1 small onion, peeled and finely chopped
1 small garlic clove, peeled and minced
$^1\!/_2$ teaspoon finely grated fresh ginger
$^1\!/_4$ teaspoon ground turmeric
$^1\!/_4$ teaspoon Garam Masala (see below)
$^1\!/_2$ cup red lentils, washed and drained
$^2\!/_3$ cup Chicken Stock (see page 235)
Salt
Freshly ground black pepper

Four 12 x 17-inch sheets phyllo dough
Approximately $^1\!/_2$ cup canola (or other vegetable) oil for preparing dough

Heat 2 teaspoons oil in a small saucepan over medium heat. Add onion, garlic, and ginger. Sauté, stirring occasionally, until onion is golden brown. Stir in turmeric and Garam Masala. Add lentils. Stir and cook 2 minutes.

Pour in Chicken Stock. Stir to combine. Bring to a boil. Reduce heat to a simmer. Cover pan and cook lentils until liquid has been absorbed and lentils are very soft, about 20 minutes. Add salt and pepper to taste. Set aside to cool.

Preheat oven to 375 degrees.

When lentil mixture is cool, prepare phyllo dough. Place one sheet of dough on a dry work surface with the longer dimension running horizontally. Brush dough with oil. Lay a second sheet of phyllo on top of the first, in the same fashion. Brush this piece of dough with oil. Using a very sharp knife, trim edges so all sides are neat and free from cracks.

Cut dough vertically into six 2½-inch-wide strips. Place about 1 tablespoon of the lentil mixture near one end of the pastry strip. Fold the end of the dough diagonally over the lentils, thereby forming a triangle at that end. Fold again and again, keeping the triangular shape, until pastry strip is completely wrapped around lentil filling. Brush top of pastry triangle with more oil and place on a sheet pan lined with aluminum foil.

Repeat this process with the remaining filling and phyllo until there are 12 samosas.

Place the sheet pan in the center of the preheated oven. Bake until the samosas are golden brown, 15–20 minutes.

To serve, place 2 samosas on a small plate with triangle tips touching at the center of the plate. Place a mound of Mango Chutney and a mound of Eggplant Pickle on opposite sides of triangle points in the center of the plate. Serve immediately.

Yield: 12 samosas

Note: Samosas can be assembled ahead of time and kept tightly covered in the refrigerator for 1 day. Brush them with oil again before baking. They may also be frozen, before baking, for several months. To cook frozen samosas, remove from freezer, place on a sheet pan lined with aluminum foil, brush tops with additional oil, and bake as above, allowing a few additional minutes of cooking time.

2 samosas (without condiments)
Cholesterol: 0 mg   Total Fat: 13 gm
Saturated Fat: 1 gm   Calories: 272

GARAM MASALA

Garam masala is a traditional North Indian blend of highly aromatic spices, dry-roasted and ground, that forms the basis for the taste we recognize as "Indian." The following mixture is uniquely ours and will keep its mighty flavor for a year.

  4 teaspoons ground coriander
  1 tablespoon ground cumin
  2 teaspoons freshly ground black pepper
  1 teaspoon ground cardamom

1 teaspoon ground cinnamon
$^1/_2$ teaspoon ground cloves
$^1/_2$ teaspoon ground nutmeg

Place all the spices in a dry, heavy-bottomed frying pan. Heat over medium flame until spices become fragrant and are lightly toasted, about 5 minutes. (Stir spices occasionally to prevent burning.) Remove Garam Masala to a small bowl and allow to cool.

Yield: 4 tablespoons

Note: Store in an airtight jar up to 1 year.

Cholesterol: 0 mg	Total Fat: 0 gm
Saturated Fat: 0 gm	Calories: 0

Mango Chutney

This delicious fruit chutney, full of sugar and spice, makes a great gift. It's a winner with cocktails, served with Yogurt Cheese (see page 239) and water biscuits. And it can be used in a different and appealing salad entrée. Just combine a small amount of it with cubed poultry, sliced and toasted almonds, a dollop of Mayonnaise (ours, of course; see page 238), and a dash of curry powder.

2 medium firm mangoes (about $^3/_4$ pound each), peeled, seeded, and cubed
$^3/_4$ teaspoon salt
1 large jalapeño pepper, seeded and coarsely chopped
2 medium garlic cloves, peeled and minced
1 tablespoon finely chopped fresh ginger
$^3/_4$ cup malt vinegar
1 cinnamon stick, 3 inches long
1 cup granulated sugar
$^1/_2$ teaspoon ground cumin
$^1/_4$ cup dried currants

Mix mango with salt in a small bowl and set aside.

Combine jalapeño pepper, garlic, ginger, vinegar, cinnamon stick, sugar, and cumin in a medium saucepan and simmer 15 minutes.

Add mango and currants and cook until mixture becomes thick, about 30 minutes.

Remove from heat and cool completely before storing in an airtight jar.

Yield: About 2½ cups

Note: Chutney will keep several weeks in the refrigerator in an airtight container.

2 tablespoons
Cholesterol: 0 mg   Total Fat: 0 gm
Saturated Fat: 0 gm   Calories: 56

Eggplant Pickle

The fascinating and exotic flavor of this homemade Indian pickle will intrigue your guests. Ours can never figure out just what they're eating, so the first course becomes a guessing game and an icebreaker.

1 large eggplant (about 1 pound), peeled and cut into ½-inch cubes

1 teaspoon salt

3 tablespoons canola (or other vegetable) oil

1 teaspoon ground turmeric

2 teaspoons black mustard seeds

1 tablespoon curry powder

¼ cup malt vinegar

2 teaspoons dark brown sugar

1 large onion, peeled and diced

2 large garlic cloves, peeled and coarsely chopped

2 teaspoons finely chopped fresh ginger

2 tablespoons freshly squeezed lime juice, strained

2 small jalapeño peppers, seeded and coarsely chopped

Toss cubed eggplant with salt. Set aside in a colander to drain at least 1 hour. Pat dry with paper toweling.

Heat oil in a large nonstick skillet over high flame until it just begins to smoke. Stir in eggplant. Lower heat to medium and cook, stirring frequently, until eggplant is evenly browned. Remove eggplant from pan with a slotted spoon and drain on paper towels. Discard any oil remaining in skillet and wipe it dry.

Using the same pan, heat the turmeric, mustard seeds, and curry powder over medium heat, stirring frequently, until the spices begin to brown and the mustard seeds begin to pop (this will take a minute or so).

Add the vinegar, sugar, onion, garlic, ginger, lime juice, and jalapeño peppers. Simmer until liquid evaporates, about 7 minutes. Add the cooked eggplant and sauté until very tender, about 10 minutes more.

Remove mixture to a bowl and allow to cool to room temperature. Cover bowl with plastic wrap and refrigerate.

To serve, remove Eggplant Pickle from refrigerator and allow to stand at room temperature at least 2 hours before serving.

Yield: About 2 cups

Note: Eggplant Pickle will keep in the refrigerator 2–3 weeks, covered tightly.

2 tablespoons
Cholesterol: 0 mg   Total Fat: 3 gm
Saturated Fat: 0.2 gm   Calories: 38

Shrimp and Potato Curry

The first party I ever catered was for my father's birthday. I was eight years old. I served canapés fashioned from white bread and cream cheese dyed with food coloring. My next culinary effort was sautéed veal kidneys. I found them a great success, but the rest of the family got a whiff of them and asked me to turn in my apron. I didn't get another chance at the stove until I left home. In an apartment lit with candles stuck in Chianti bottles and decorated with Indian bedspreads, my roommates and I cooked curry and discussed the cosmos (it was the sixties). I'm still wild about that hot, spicy, richly sauced fare. It's fun food and makes for a great party.

Serve the curry family-style and pass the condiments.

2 pounds raw shrimp
2 tablespoons finely chopped fresh coriander (cilantro)
Juice and finely grated zest of 1 lime
2 cups water
1 cup dry vermouth
1 bay leaf
6 black peppercorns
2 tablespoons canola (or other vegetable) oil
2 large onions, peeled and diced
6 large garlic cloves, peeled and minced
3 tablespoons curry powder
1 teaspoon ground cumin
1½ pounds boiling potatoes, peeled and cut into ½-inch cubes
½ cup green peas, fresh or frozen
Salt
Freshly ground black pepper

Peel and devein shrimp, reserving shells. In a bowl, combine fresh coriander, lime juice, and zest to make a marinade. Add shrimp and stir to coat. Cover with plastic wrap and refrigerate till needed.

Meanwhile, make a shrimp stock. Place reserved shrimp shells in a large pot with water, vermouth, bay leaf, and peppercorns. Bring to a boil over high heat. Lower heat and simmer until liquid is reduced to 2 cups, about 1 hour. Strain and reserve liquid.

In a large, deep skillet, heat oil over high flame and sauté onions, stirring constantly, until translucent, 5–6 minutes. Add garlic and sauté until onions start to brown, 4–5 minutes longer. Sprinkle in the curry powder and cumin, stirring to coat onions. Add potatoes and peas, stirring until all ingredients are well combined.

Pour in shrimp stock. Bring to a boil. Cover and lower flame. Simmer slowly until potatoes are tender, stirring occasionally, 25–30 minutes. Uncover, add shrimp and marinade and salt and pepper to taste. Cook until shrimp are done, about 10 minutes.

Cholesterol: 176 mg   Total Fat: 7 gm
Saturated Fat: 1 gm   Calories: 303

Mint and Coriander Raita

A raita is a cool yogurt salad or relish. It is a classic accompaniment to curry dishes, because of its ability to soothe the palate. It is usually made with whole milk yogurt, but loses none of its taste in our nonfat rendition. Try it mixed with chunks of chicken breast (no skin, please) and hefty cucumber cubes for a refreshing summer salad.

One 16-ounce container plain nonfat yogurt
4 teaspoons finely chopped fresh coriander (cilantro)
2 teaspoons finely chopped fresh mint

Drain excess liquid from yogurt. Combine yogurt with coriander and mint. Stir with a whisk until evenly blended. Cover tightly with plastic wrap and refrigerate at least 1 hour before serving.

Yield: 2 cups
Note: Raita will keep 5–6 days in the refrigerator.

¹/₃ cup
Cholesterol: 1 mg   Total Fat: 0 gm
Saturated Fat: 0 gm   Calories: 42

Carrot-Cucumber Sambal

A sambal is a common accompaniment found throughout southern India, Indonesia, and Malaysia. It is one of a group of dishes that are served alongside the fiery foods of these regions as both antidote and complement to the fire of the chilies that give this food its characteristic kick. We add carrots to the usual cucumbers for the sweetness and color they provide. With the addition of some jumbo shrimp, this makes an excellent luncheon dish.

3 medium cucumbers, peeled, seeded, and cubed
$\frac{1}{2}$ teaspoon salt
Juice and finely grated zest of 2 small limes
2 teaspoons granulated sugar
1 small garlic clove, peeled and minced
$\frac{1}{8}$ teaspoon cayenne pepper
2 medium carrots, peeled, quartered lengthwise, and sliced crosswise $\frac{1}{4}$ inch thick

Toss cucumber pieces with salt and set aside in a colander to drain at least 1 hour.

Combine lime juice and zest, sugar, garlic, and cayenne pepper in a medium bowl. Stir to blend.

Add the cucumber and carrot pieces, mixing well. Cover bowl tightly with plastic wrap and refrigerate for several hours before serving.

Yield: About $3\frac{1}{2}$ cups

Note: The sambal will keep for 1 day in the refrigerator.

Cholesterol: 0 mg   Total Fat: 0 gm
Saturated Fat: 0 gm   Calories: 22

Spiced Pita Bread

An appealing feature of Indian fare is the variety of fantastic breads made to be eaten with the curries. But those parathas and pooris are either brushed with butter and fried on griddles or deep-fried in buckets of oil. We couldn't serve this meal without something to sop up the sauce, so we invented this. We use pita, a Middle Eastern flat bread widely available in grocery stores and supermarkets, and give it a homemade quality by adorning it with a variety of traditional Indian spices.

1 tablespoon fenugreek seeds
$^3/_4$ teaspoon fennel seeds
$1^1/_2$ teaspoons cumin seeds
$1^1/_2$ teaspoons black mustard seeds
$2^1/_2$ teaspoons Garam Masala (see page 49)
6 tablespoons canola (or other vegetable) oil
9 pita breads (1 ounce each)

Preheat oven to 275 degrees.

Place fenugreek, fennel, cumin, and mustard seeds in a blender or food processor. Pulse several times to crack seeds. Remove to a small bowl and stir in Garam Masala. Set aside.

In a large nonstick frying pan, heat 2 teaspoons oil and 1 teaspoon spice mixture over high heat. When seeds begin to pop, add one pita bread, frying it on each side until lightly browned, about 3 minutes total. Remove to a sheet pan and grill remaining pita breads in the same manner.

Cover the sheet pan holding the fried breads with aluminum foil and place in the center of the preheated oven. Keep warm until ready to serve.

Note: The breads should be held no longer than 15 minutes in the oven, to prevent their drying out.

1 pita
Cholesterol: 0 mg   Total Fat: 10 gm
Saturated Fat: 1 gm   Calories: 148

Tropical Fruit Salad with Candied Ginger

This interesting and refreshing dessert comes from Onda, a New York restaurant owned by Karen Hubert and Len Allison, a couple long known for their innovative cooking style. A creation of chef Nina Fraas, it combines a mixture of common and exotic fruits with the mellow flavor of honey, the intriguing taste of candied ginger, and the pep and freshness of mint. The result is the perfect ending to this Indian meal.

½ cup honey (clover or other light variety)

¼ cup finely chopped candied ginger

Juice and finely grated zest of 1 lime

12 fresh mint leaves, finely chopped

1 large pineapple, peeled, cored, and cut into ½-inch pieces (reserve any juice)

1 large mango, peeled, pitted, and cut into ½-inch pieces (reserve any juice)

2 small kiwis, peeled and cut into ½-inch pieces (reserve any juice)

3 large blood oranges, peeled, white pith removed, and separated into individual sections (reserve any juice)

2 small grapefruits, peeled, white pith removed, and separated into individual sections (reserve any juice)

In a small saucepan, heat the honey over low flame until warm, 3–4 minutes. Add the ginger, lime juice and zest, and mint leaves. Set aside.

In a medium bowl, place pineapple, mango, kiwi, orange, grapefruit, all reserved juice, and the honey mixture. Stir to combine, place, and refrigerate at least ½ hour before using.

To serve, retoss fruit and juice and place in an attractive serving bowl.

Cholesterol: 0 mg   Total Fat: 0 gm
Saturated Fat: 0 gm   Calories: 227

Thanksgiving

Serves 6

Several-Squash Soup
Roast Turkey
Good Gravy
Baked Bread Stuffing
Cranberry-Citrus Relish
Caramelized Onions
Sautéed Brussels Leaves
American Apple Pie

Several-Squash Soup

Thanksgiving dinner is my favorite meal of the year — the more traditional the better. It has to start with pumpkin soup, which in the old days meant a little pumpkin, a lot of butter, and oodles of cream. Nowadays, we keep the savory essence of the soup by combining the flavors of three different seasonal squashes with a couple of surprising ingredients like brown sugar and curry powder. We've changed the cream to nonfat yogurt, taken out the butter, and kept every bit of the flavor. Bring this soup to the table using a hollow pumpkin as your tureen, or ladle it into miniature pumpkin shells instead of bowls.

1 small pie pumpkin, halved and seeded
1 small butternut squash, halved and seeded
1 small acorn squash, halved and seeded
1 tablespoon canola (or other vegetable) oil
5 large carrots, peeled and finely chopped
2 small shallots, peeled and finely chopped
1 tablespoon dark brown sugar
$\frac{1}{2}$ teaspoon curry powder
$\frac{1}{4}$ teaspoon freshly grated nutmeg
1 tablespoon all-purpose flour
5 cups Chicken Stock (see page 235)
1 cup plain nonfat yogurt
Salt
Freshly ground black pepper
Finely chopped fresh chives

Preheat oven to 375 degrees.

In a large roasting pan to which 1 inch of water has been added place pumpkin and squash halves cut side down. Cover pan tightly with aluminum foil and bake until vegetables become soft, and can be easily pierced with a knife, about 50 minutes. Remove from oven. Set vegetables aside until cool enough to handle comfortably.

Scrape flesh from the skin of each vegetable and puree each separately in a food processor. Measure 1 cup of each puree and set aside. (Any remaining puree may be reserved for another use.)

Heat oil in a large saucepan (about 4-quart capacity) over medium heat. Add carrots, shallots, and brown sugar. Cover pot with lid and cook, stirring occasionally, until carrots are tender, about 15 minutes.

Uncover pot, add curry powder, nutmeg, and flour. Stir and cook for 1 minute. Add Chicken Stock and pumpkin and squash purees. Stir until well combined. Allow mixture to come to a slow boil. Reduce heat and simmer, uncovered, for 15 minutes.

Add the yogurt and salt and pepper to taste and simmer 15 minutes longer. Remove from heat and cool slightly.

In small batches, puree the mixture in a food processor until smooth. Force the puree through a fine sieve, discarding solids that remain. To serve, heat the soup to a simmer in a large saucepan. Taste and adjust seasoning if necessary.

Portion the soup into 6 warmed bowls and sprinkle chives on top. Serve immediately.

Yield: About 2½ quarts.

Note: The soup may be made several days in advance and stored in an airtight container in the refrigerator. It can also be frozen for several weeks.

Cholesterol: 1 mg   Total Fat: 5 gm
Saturated Fat: 0 gm   Calories: 154

Roast Turkey

I love turkey. As soon as I became old enough to carve, I would volunteer for the job just so I could be alone in the kitchen with the coveted bird. There I would peel off and eat as much skin as I could get away with. I'd also sample the tiny medallions of dark meat nearest the backbone, the buttery juices running down my arm.

Is there life after turkey skin? Try this recipe and see!

One 8-to-10-pound freshly killed turkey
2 teaspoons salt
2 teaspoons freshly ground black pepper
2 teaspoons ground sage

2 teaspoons ground coriander
1 small onion, peeled and coarsely chopped
2 medium celery ribs, coarsely chopped
1 large carrot, peeled and coarsely chopped
2 medium garlic cloves, peeled and coarsely chopped
Extra-virgin olive oil for basting turkey

Preheat oven to 350 degrees.

Wash the turkey inside and out with cool water. Pat dry with paper toweling. Tuck wings under the turkey's back, so they stay in place.

To facilitate skinning the turkey later, make a cut through the skin and tendons, deep to the bone, completely around each drumstick, just below its fleshy part.

In a small bowl, combine the salt, pepper, sage, and coriander. Rub this mixture all over the inside of the turkey, both body cavity and neck cavity.

In another bowl, combine onion, celery, carrot, and garlic. Loosely stuff the body cavity with this mixture. (These vegetables are used for seasoning the turkey and are not intended for consumption.) Use butcher's cord to tie together the crossed legs and tail. (Or use small metal skewers to do this.)

Place the turkey, breast side up, on a rack in a roasting pan. Lightly brush the skin all over with olive oil to achieve an attractive browned skin for presentation. Place the turkey in the preheated oven and roast for about 15 minutes per pound, basting with pan juices every 20 minutes. After 30 minutes, carefully turn the bird onto its side. After another 30 minutes, turn the bird onto its other side. Thirty minutes later, return the bird to its back for the remainder of the roasting time.

When the bird is done (juices from the interior of the thigh should be clear, not pink), take it from the oven and remove the butcher's cord or skewers. Should you wish to present the turkey before carving, do so in its browned, "skin-on" state. The meat should be served, however, without its skin or fatty parts.

Before carving, remove the wings. To remove the skin from the breast, first make a cut just through the skin, lengthwise, from the tip of the breastbone to the center of the wishbone. Next, cut the skin completely around the thighs to release them from the sides of the breast. The skin should easily lift away from the breast at this time.

To remove the skin from the legs and thighs, cut through the skin from the edge that was just released from the breast, along the length of the thigh and drumstick, until you reach the collar that was cut around each drumstick before roasting. This should allow you to easily pull the skin away from the dark meat.

5 ounces, mixed white and dark meat
Cholesterol: 136 mg   Total Fat: 5 gm
Saturated Fat: 1 gm   Calories: 232

Good Gravy

Good gravy is an essential part of this Thanksgiving meal. The confirmed cholesterol-minded among your guests will be strictly white-meat eaters. And the breast meat, even at its juiciest, demands a savory sauce. This is an opportunity for one of your stocks to shine. Have them on hand, and this do-ahead job becomes a breeze. When it comes time for dinner, don't be surprised at how often you hear "Please pass the gravy."

1/2 cup dry white wine
3 cups Brown Chicken Stock (see page 235), reduced to 1 1/2 cups
2 tablespoons arrowroot mixed with 1/2 cup water to form a paste
2 teaspoons finely minced fresh sage leaves
2 teaspoons finely minced fresh parsley
Salt
Freshly ground black pepper

After removing the turkey and rack from the roasting pan, discard all pan juices and fat.

On high heat atop the stove, add the wine to the roasting pan. As the wine boils, scrape the caramelized juices from the bottom of the pan. When the wine has reduced by about half, add the Brown Chicken Stock. Let the stock come to a complete boil, then whisk in the arrowroot paste. Blend thoroughly. When the gravy has nearly regained its boil, it will have thickened and must be removed from the heat. (See note.)

Strain the gravy. Mix in the sage and parsley. Season to taste with salt and pepper and serve immediately.

Yield: Scant 2 cups

Note: Care must be taken when reheating sauces thickened with arrowroot. Never allow the sauce to regain a full boil; heat to just under a boil. Also, a skin will form on the sauce if it is allowed to cool; remove this skin before attempting to reheat the sauce.

2 tablespoons
Cholesterol: 0 mg   Total Fat: 1 gm
Saturated Fat: 0.5 gm   Calories: 18

Baked Bread Stuffing

Stuffing is a subject about which everyone has a strong opinion. Memory foods are like that. So for me, in my former cooking life, the only way to go was to start with the same packaged mix my mother always used. I'd follow the directions (which included lots of melted butter) and add fruit, vegetables, sausage, and liver (sautéed in even more butter) just the way she did. The result, while tasty, was a killer. These days, we cut the fat while keeping a lot of the qualities that made the original stuffing so memorable.

2 tablespoons extra-virgin olive oil
$^1\!/_2$ cup chopped ($^1\!/_2$-inch dice) celery
$^1\!/_2$ cup chopped ($^1\!/_2$-inch dice) onion
$^1\!/_2$ cup chopped ($^1\!/_2$-inch dice) carrot
$^1\!/_2$ cup dried currants
$^1\!/_2$ teaspoon ground cinnamon
$^1\!/_2$ teaspoon ground coriander
1 teaspoon salt
$^1\!/_2$ teaspoon freshly ground black pepper
2 teaspoons minced fresh sage leaves
$^1\!/_2$ cup finely chopped fresh parsley
5 cups soft bread cubes
2 cups Chicken Stock (see page 235), brought to a boil
5 large egg whites, at room temperature

Preheat oven to 350 degrees.

In a saucepan, combine oil, celery, onion, carrot, currants, cinnamon, coriander, salt, and pepper. Cook over medium heat until onions are soft and somewhat transparent.

Combine cooked vegetables and their liquid in a large bowl with sage, parsley, bread cubes, and Chicken Stock.

Beat egg whites until they form stiff peaks. Gently fold them into the bread mixture. Turn into a 13 x 9 x 2-inch ovenproof dish; place this in a larger pan into which you've poured enough warm water to come up 1 inch on side of baking dish. Bake for 45 minutes.

Serve hot.

Cholesterol: 0 mg	Total Fat: 6 gm
Saturated Fat: 1 gm	Calories: 212

Cranberry-Citrus Relish

No Thanksgiving meal would be complete without cranberry sauce. In a pinch you can open a can of the jellied stuff. Nobody will mind, since you have nostalgia on your side. But if you have the time, try this beautiful relish. It's a cut above the usual cranberry-orange mélange. The addition of lemons and onion take it out of the ordinary, while the ginger, garlic, vinegar, and brown sugar add a nice kick and some welcome sweetness. Whip up another batch on a rainy Sunday, and ladle it into sterilized jars for a wonderful seasonal gift.

1 medium lemon
1 medium orange
1 pound cranberries
1 cup finely chopped onion
2 tablespoons minced fresh or candied ginger
1 tablespoon minced garlic
$\frac{1}{4}$ cup apple cider vinegar
$\frac{1}{4}$ cup brown sugar
$\frac{1}{4}$ teaspoon nutmeg
1 cinnamon stick

Grate the rinds of the lemon and orange. Reserve. Cut away and discard the skin and pith. Cut fruit segments from their membranes and chop the flesh. Discard seeds and membranes.

In a saucepan, combine the grated rind and chopped fruit with all the other ingredients. Stirring over high heat, bring to a boil. Immediately reduce heat and maintain a simmer for about 45 minutes.

Cool thoroughly before refrigerating.

Yield: 3 cups

Note: Relish may be made up to 1 week in advance and kept in the refrigerator.

¹/₄ cup

Cholesterol: 0 mg	Total Fat: 0 gm
Saturated Fat: 0 gm	Calories: 43

Caramelized Onions

Creamed onions, a regular feature of many Thanksgiving dinners, have to go. Why not try something new like these onions, with their rich, meaty flavor. They're light, and even with seconds you'll have room for dessert.

2 tablespoons canola (or other vegetable) oil
2 pounds uniformly small white onions, peeled
2 tablespoons bourbon
1 cup Brown Chicken Stock (see page 235)
2 tablespoons molasses
¹/₂ teaspoon salt

Heat the oil in a sauté pan. Add the onions. Stir-fry just to brown them. Transfer onions to paper toweling and blot away surface oil.

In a saucepan large enough to hold all the onions, combine them with the bourbon, chicken stock, molasses, and salt.

Simmer covered over low heat, stirring occasionally, until the onions are tender, about 30 minutes. Uncover and continue to cook over medium-high heat, stirring frequently. Remove from heat when the only liquid remaining is the glaze on the onions.

Cholesterol: 0 mg   Total Fat: 11 gm
Saturated Fat: 2 gm   Calories: 131

Sautéed Brussels Leaves

My friend Marianne Melendez came up with the inspiration for this recipe. She had found a stalk of brussels sprouts at her local farmers' market, and having denuded it, just kept on going. She took each leaf off every sprout, blanched the lot, and sautéed the result in lots of sweet butter. Nobody could quite figure out what we were eating, but we were enchanted, nonetheless. For your Thanksgiving table, we keep the concept but eliminate the cholesterol. We've already fooled lots of people who can't stand this vegetable. You will too.

3 pints fresh brussels sprouts, washed and trimmed of damaged leaves
1 tablespoon canola (or other vegetable) oil
1 tablespoon walnut oil
One 3 1/2-ounce package fresh enoki mushrooms, washed and trimmed
2 small shallots, peeled and very thinly sliced
1/8 teaspoon ground cloves
Salt
Freshly ground black pepper

Cut and separate the leaves from the stems of each brussels sprout.

In a deep pot, bring 4 quarts water to a rapid boil over high heat. Add the sprout leaves. Stir them into the boiling water. Continue to stir for 1 minute. Drain the leaves in a colander.

Immediately transfer the leaves to a large bowl containing 2 quarts of cold water and 1 pound of ice to prevent further cooking. Once the leaves have cooled, drain them again. Dry thoroughly.

In a sauté pan large enough to hold all the ingredients, heat the canola and walnut oils. Add the brussels sprout leaves, enoki mushrooms, and shallots.

Sprinkle in the ground cloves. Stir-fry for about 2 minutes. Season with salt and pepper.

Cholesterol: 0 mg   Total Fat: 5 gm
Saturated Fat: 0.4 gm Calories: 83

American Apple Pie

I've never met an apple dessert I didn't like. And what's more fitting than the all-American apple pie to end this holiday meal? In our version the butter- or lard-based pastry is replaced by one of our own invention, designed to eliminate all that unhealthy fat. We use oil and yogurt instead, and still end up with a rich, flaky crust. We like Granny Smiths for our apples, but any firm, tart apple will do.

For the pastry:

2 cups all-purpose flour
1/4 cup granulated sugar
1 teaspoon salt
1/2 cup plus 2 tablespoons canola (or other vegetable) oil
1/4 cup plain nonfat yogurt

For the filling:

6 cups peeled, cored, and thinly sliced apples (Granny Smith or Winesap)
1/3 cup granulated sugar
1/3 cup light brown sugar
Pinch of salt
1 teaspoon ground cinnamon
1 tablespoon finely grated lemon rind
1 tablespoon freshly squeezed lemon juice, strained
1 tablespoon cornstarch

For finishing the pie:

1 large egg white
1 tablespoon water
Granulated sugar for dusting the top

To make the pastry, place flour, sugar, and salt in a medium-size bowl. Stir with a whisk to combine. Make a well in the center of the dry ingredients. Add the oil and yogurt and stir them together. Quickly work the dry ingredients into the liquid, just until the mixture forms a ball.

Divide the dough into two equal balls. Flatten to form circles about 1 inch thick. Wrap each in plastic and refrigerate for 1 hour.

To make the filling, combine the apple slices with the granulated sugar, brown sugar, salt, cinnamon, lemon rind, lemon juice, and cornstarch. Toss to coat the apple slices evenly. Set aside.

Preheat oven to 425 degrees.

To assemble the pie, remove the dough from the refrigerator. Discard plastic wrap. Place each circle of dough between two sheets of wax paper. Roll the dough into circles about 11–12 inches in diameter and of uniform thickness, between $1/8$ inch and $1/4$ inch thick. Remove each top layer of wax paper. Invert one piece of dough into a 9-inch pie plate. Press the dough into place, then remove wax paper.

Turn the apple filling into the pie shell.

Make an egg wash by lightly beating the egg white with 1 tablespoon of water. Brush the part of the dough that rests on the lip of the pie plate with egg wash. Invert the second piece of dough over the filled pie. Remove wax paper. Trim any excess dough from the sides. Seal and flute the edges. Sparingly brush the entire top of the pie with egg wash. Dust with granulated sugar, brushing off any excess. Make several slits in the top crust.

Bake in the middle of the preheated oven until the crust is browned, about 50 minutes.

Allow to cool thoroughly before serving. Reheat pie if you wish to serve it warm.

Cholesterol: 0 mg   Total Fat: 19 gm
Saturated Fat: 2 gm   Calories: 413

WINTER

A Warm-up Breakfast

Serves 6

Mulled Wine

Willa's Waffles

Rhubarb Sauce

Whipped Yogurt Cream

Smoked Salmon Sausages

Carrot-Spice Cake

Really Rum Sauce

Mulled Wine

What better accompaniment to this winter brunch than a soothing, hot, spicy brew. Serve this robust red wine flavored with fruit and winter spices in generous mugs. Your guests will feel so warm and cozy, you'll have a hard time getting them back out in the cold when the party's over.

6 cups dry red wine
6 whole cloves
2 cinnamon sticks, broken into several pieces
1 large apple, cored and cut into 1-inch pieces
1 medium lemon, cut in half, seeds removed
1 large orange, zest removed with a vegetable peeler and cut into strips, white pith discarded, fruit cut into 1-inch pieces

In a large pot, combine all the ingredients and bring to a boil. Remove from heat and discard orange peel, cloves, and cinnamon sticks.

Serve hot, making sure to put some fruit in each mug.

Note: May be sweetened with sugar to taste, if desired.

Cholesterol: 0 mg   Total Fat: 0 gm
Saturated Fat: 0 gm   Calories: 220

Willa's Waffles

I'm a morning person. My favorite meal is breakfast. I spent my life as a two-egg-a-day girl until the cholesterol police caught up with me. I was floundering from muffin to muesli when I discovered a no-cholesterol waffle in my supermarket. It was warm and soft, sweet and soothing. I liked it. But I couldn't serve it to clients. They didn't need me to open a box. Besides, if the supermarket version was good, we could make it better. Several waffle irons and hundreds of waffle hours later, here it is. Top it with Rhubarb Sauce (next recipe) and add some Whipped Yogurt Cream (page 240) alongside for a taste of spring in midwinter.

1½ cups all-purpose flour

¼ cup whole wheat flour

¼ cup yellow cornmeal

½ teaspoon salt

1 teaspoon baking powder

½ teaspoon baking soda

1 tablespoon granulated sugar

2 cups low-fat buttermilk

1 teaspoon pure vanilla extract

2 tablespoons dark brown sugar

3 tablespoons canola (or other vegetable) oil, plus extra oil to grease waffle iron

2 large egg whites, at room temperature

Oil and preheat waffle iron.

Into a large bowl sift together both flours, cornmeal, salt, baking powder, baking soda, and granulated sugar. Set aside.

In a small bowl combine the buttermilk, vanilla extract, brown sugar, and 3 tablespoons oil. Stir until the sugar dissolves. Set aside.

Whip the egg whites until they form soft peaks. Briefly set them aside while combining the other ingredients.

Make a well in the center of the dry ingredients. Add the buttermilk mixture to the well and stir to combine liquid and dry ingredients, just until a smooth batter forms. Add beaten egg whites and fold into the batter.

Pour enough batter onto the hot waffle iron to make 1 waffle. Cook to desired doneness. Three to four minutes will yield a soft, slightly doughy waffle. Cook for an extra minute if you prefer a crisp, dry waffle.

Yield: 6 waffles (6–7-inch diameter)

Cholesterol: 3 mg	Total Fat: 8 gm
Saturated Fat: 1 gm	Calories: 272

Rhubarb Sauce

Rhubarb is seriously underappreciated. Okay, a fruit that's really a vegetable and looks like red celery is confusing. But it's worth getting acquainted with this quirky crop. It makes a great sauce with its unique sweet-and-sour taste. And it adds complexity to the straightforwardness of the waffle that it accompanies. Keep some extra on hand as a versatile dessert sauce.

4 cups rhubarb stems, washed and cut into ¼-inch pieces
¾ cup granulated sugar
2 teaspoons pure vanilla extract
½ teaspoon ground cinnamon

Combine rhubarb, sugar, vanilla extract, and cinnamon in a medium saucepan (about 2-quart capacity). Place over low flame and stir until sugar dissolves, 1–2 minutes. Cover pan with lid.

Stirring occasionally, allow mixture to simmer until rhubarb becomes very tender and begins to break into fibers when stirred, 15–20 minutes.

Remove from heat. Uncover pan and transfer rhubarb to a serving bowl. Serve warm or at room temperature.

Yield: About 3 cups

Note: Sauce can be made several days ahead and stored in an airtight container in the refrigerator. It can be frozen for several months, so consider making a large batch in summertime, when rhubarb is plentiful.

2 *tablespoons*
Cholesterol: 0 mg   Total Fat: 0 gm
Saturated Fat: 0 gm   Calories: 28

Smoked Salmon Sausages

These little wursts are a hit at any party. The element of surprise that registers with the first mouthful, when they are not what they seem, works every time. And their subtle, smoky flavor provides a delicious contrast to the soft, sweet taste of the waffles and Rhubarb Sauce. Buy the best smoked fish you can afford. Quality really counts here.

8 ounces smoked salmon, coarsely chopped
4 large egg whites
2 cups fine bread crumbs, made from fresh Portuguese-Style Sweet Bread
    (see page 138) or other no-cholesterol bread
Canola (or other vegetable) oil

Place salmon and egg whites in the workbowl of a food processor. Using short pulses, puree until salmon is finely ground.

Add bread crumbs and continue to pulse just to combine. Remove mixture to a small bowl. Cover tightly with plastic wrap. Refrigerate for 30 minutes.

Fill a medium saucepan (about 2-quart capacity) half full with water. Heat over medium flame to just below the boiling point.

While the water is heating, remove salmon mixture from the refrigerator. Put it into a pastry bag fitted with a ¾-inch plain tip. Force the mixture through the tube onto a sheet of wax paper to form a log about 3 inches long. Use a sharp knife to sever the mixture from the pastry tip. Continue until 12 sausages are formed. Refrigerate.

When the water is ready, gently place 4 sausages at a time into the water (leave the rest in the refrigerator). Poach until they become opaque and float to the top, about 5 minutes.

Remove sausages from water with a slotted spoon and reserve on a plate. Repeat process with remaining sausages, making sure the water never boils. (Boiling water will cause them to lose their shape.)

When all the sausages have been poached, cover them with plastic wrap and refrigerate at least 30 minutes, or until ready to serve.

To serve, heat a few drops of oil in a large nonstick frying pan (about 12 inches in diameter) over high heat. Rotating sausages, fry on all sides until brown and crisp, 5–6 minutes. Remove from pan and serve on a warm plate.

Yield: 12 sausages

Note: Once the sausages have been poached, they can be stored, tightly wrapped, in the refrigerator up to 24 hours.

2 sausages
Cholesterol: 9 mg   Total Fat: 5 gm
Saturated Fat: 1 gm   Calories: 124

Carrot-Spice Cake

Early in my catering career, I had the good fortune to meet a fascinating and dynamic public relations woman, Alice Fixx, whose suggestions and generosity were most helpful. Her greatest contribution, however, was introducing me to a talented young pastry chef, my collaborator, Greg Case, who has since become a treasured friend and priceless colleague. He still makes a 14-karat cake, but one that can now be enjoyed by the cholesterol-conscious. Gone is the cream cheese icing, but not to worry. The Really Rum Sauce (see next recipe) that has taken its place will warm your healthy heart.

Solid vegetable shortening to grease baking pan
Flour to dust baking pan
1 pound carrots, peeled and dried
2 cups all-purpose flour
1 teaspoon salt
1 teaspoon ground cinnamon
$1/4$ teaspoon ground allspice
$1/4$ teaspoon ground mace
$1/2$ teaspoon ground cloves
2 teaspoons baking soda
1 cup canola (or other vegetable) oil
6 large egg whites
$1/2$ cup dark brown sugar
1 cup granulated sugar
$1/2$ cup dried currants, plumped in warm water and drained

Preheat oven to 350 degrees.

Grease and flour an 8-cup-capacity tube pan. Invert and tap pan to remove excess flour. Set aside.

Cut carrots into 1-inch pieces and grind in food processor until they become the size of coarse cornmeal. (Carrots can alternatively be grated by hand, using a fine blade.) Set aside.

In a large bowl, sift together flour, salt, cinnamon, allspice, mace, cloves, and baking soda. Set aside.

In a medium bowl combine oil, egg whites, and both sugars. Stir with a whisk, mashing any lumps of brown sugar, until a smooth batter is obtained. Set aside.

Make a well in the center of the dry ingredients. Pour in the oil–egg white batter. Stir until homogenous. Add carrots and stir. Add currants. Mix until all ingredients are evenly blended.

Pour the batter into the prepared tube pan. Bake in the center of the preheated oven until cake springs back when pressed in center and a toothpick inserted into the center of the cake comes out clean, 60–65 minutes.

Remove cake from oven and cool on a wire rack for 15 minutes. Invert pan onto rack. Tap bottom of pan to loosen cake. Lift tube pan to release cake onto rack. Finish cooling cake to room temperature before serving.

Serve individual slices on dessert plates. Pass the rum sauce in a sauceboat and let guests add their own.

Yield: 12 servings

Note: This cake, tightly covered, will keep for 5–6 days at room temperature, 2 weeks in the refrigerator, and several months in the freezer.

1 slice
Cholesterol: 0 mg   Total Fat: 18 gm
Saturated Fat: 2 gm   Calories: 373

Really Rum Sauce

6 tablespoons dark rum
1 1/2 tablespoons arrowroot
3/4 cup water
3/4 cup light brown sugar
2–3 cinnamon sticks

Combine rum and arrowroot in a small saucepan (about 4-cup capacity). Stir with a whisk to dissolve the arrowroot. Add the water, brown sugar, and cinnamon sticks and place over medium-high heat. Stir until mixture thickens and begins to boil, about 5 minutes.

Lower heat and allow to simmer, without stirring, 2–3 minutes.

Remove from heat and strain sauce. Discard the cinnamon sticks. Serve hot.

Yield: 1 1/2 cups

Note: The sauce can be kept several days in the refrigerator in an airtight container. Reheat the sauce before serving. (See note on page 63, Good Gravy, about reheating sauces thickened with arrowroot.)

2 tablespoons
Cholesterol: 0 mg   Total Fat: 0 gm
Saturated Fat: 0 gm   Calories: 55

A Fireside Lunch
Serves 6

Chicken Fricassee with Porcini
Sautéed Polenta
Grilled Fennel
Peach Amaretti Gratin

Chicken Fricassee with Porcini

We have passed the extravagant eighties and are into the no-frills nineties, and the catering business has reflected the change. Clients still entertain, but they often request simpler food that resembles the best of home cooking. Italy is a good place to look for inspiration for these recipes. Home cooks there generally use olive oil rather than butter, and the ratio of protein to other ingredients is much smaller than in this country, making the dishes healthier. A unanimous hit is our chicken with porcini mushrooms, which, as a bonus to the cook, benefits from being made in advance. A bit of the bird goes a long way, and the savory sauce flavored with the distinctive taste of the mushrooms has everyone passing their plates for seconds.

1½ ounces dried porcini mushrooms, soaked in 1 cup warm water for 20
    minutes
3 tablespoons canola (or other vegetable) oil
Two 2½-pound frying chickens, cut in serving pieces, skin removed
Salt
Freshly ground black pepper
¾ cup dry white wine
½ pound cultivated mushrooms, cleaned, stemmed, and sliced
½ cup canned Italian plum tomatoes, coarsely chopped, with their juice
1 cup Beef Stock (see page 234)
2 tablespoons Madeira

Remove porcini mushrooms from water and strain liquid through a sieve lined with a paper towel or through a paper coffee filter. Reserve liquid. Rinse the porcini thoroughly in cold running water to remove all grit. Coarsely chop and set aside.

In a large nonstick frying pan (11-inch diameter) heat the oil over medium heat. Add the chicken pieces and brown well on all sides, 10–12 minutes. Season with salt and pepper. Add the white wine and simmer, uncovered, until the liquid has evaporated, about 15 minutes. Turn the chicken once or twice while cooking.

Add the cultivated mushrooms, porcini, strained soaking liquid, tomatoes, and Beef Stock. Cover the pan with lid. Reduce heat and slowly simmer, turning chicken occasionally, until it is tender, about 30 minutes.

Uncover the pan and remove chicken to a warm platter. Raise heat to high and boil sauce until it is thick. Remove pan from heat and spoon sauce over chicken before serving.

Cholesterol: 118 mg Total Fat: 11 gm
Saturated Fat: 2 gm Calories: 309

Sautéed Polenta

I had to leave home to learn that Italians ate starches other than spaghetti and garlic bread. And I was well into my thirties before I came across polenta, a porridge made from cornmeal, popular in northern Italy. It is served either hot and mushy, or chilled until firm and cut into pieces. It can then be baked, grilled, or sautéed. Any way you choose, it's a tasty sponge to serve with a sauce, and a pleasing change from rice or noodles.

1 cup coarse yellow cornmeal
1 teaspoon salt
Pinch of cayenne pepper
$1/2$ cup cold water
4 cups Chicken Stock (see page 235)
2 tablespoons finely chopped chives
All-purpose flour for dredging
$1/4$ cup extra-virgin olive oil

Place an inch or so of water in the bottom of a double boiler and bring to a boil. Set the other half of the double boiler in place and lower the heat.

In a small bowl, combine cornmeal with salt and cayenne pepper. Add the $1/2$ cup cold water and mix thoroughly.

Bring the Chicken Stock to a full boil in a small saucepan and immediately transfer it to the top half of the double boiler. Pour in the cornmeal mixture in a steady stream, stirring constantly, and continue to stir until it is well blended with the stock. Stir in the chives, cover, and steam for 30 minutes, stirring occasionally.

Lightly oil a shallow 9 x 13-inch baking pan. Turn the polenta into the pan. Using a rubber spatula, smooth it into a uniform layer about ½ inch thick. Refrigerate uncovered until polenta becomes firm, at least 2 hours. (Once cooled, the polenta can be held, wrapped in plastic wrap, up to 1 day under refrigeration.)

Run a thin knife blade around the periphery of the pan to help loosen the polenta. Carefully invert it onto a cutting surface. Cut into 3-inch squares. Cut each square diagonally into 2 triangles.

In a shallow bowl, dust each piece of polenta with flour. Shake off any excess.

Heat the olive oil in a frying pan. Sauté polenta until uniformly brown, about 2 minutes per side.

Remove to a dish lined with paper toweling to absorb extra oil. Serve immediately.

Cholesterol: 0 mg   Total Fat: 11 gm
Saturated Fat: 1 gm   Calories: 254

Grilled Fennel

It took me a while to acquire a taste for licorice. But once I fell, I fell hard. So little wonder I flipped over fennel. As a serious fennel fan I adore it raw as a snack (sometimes going through several bulbs a day) and admire it in salads. But cook it and something magical happens. Here its rustic flavor complements the earthy goodness of the chicken fricassee. As with other grilled vegetables that we prepare, we find that blanching as a first step improves the final product, since you don't end up overcooking the outside to get it tender within.

2 large fennel bulbs, stalks removed, cut lengthwise into 6 wedges and
     blanched 5–7 minutes
2 tablespoons extra-virgin olive oil
Salt
Freshly ground black pepper

Preheat a ridged, nonstick grill pan over medium flame.

Meanwhile, rub fennel pieces with oil, salt, and pepper. When the grill begins to smoke, place several pieces of fennel on the pan. Rotate fennel to create cross-hatch marks. Turn fennel over and repeat process on other side.

Remove fennel to a platter and keep warm. Continue to cook remaining pieces in the same fashion.

Cholesterol: 0 mg   Total Fat: 7 gm
Saturated Fat: 1 gm   Calories: 50

Peach Amaretti Gratin

The idea for this dessert came from one created by our friend Pierre Prévost at Restaurant Lafayette in New York. His original was a plate of almond cream, baked with a large chocolate truffle in the middle. With all that butter and fat it was completely out of the question for us, but what we do have for you is a peach half embedded in a warm plate of almond paste — divine but not dangerous.

2 cups blanched almonds
1 cup confectioners' sugar
1 cup superfine sugar
2 tablespoons freshly squeezed lemon juice, strained
2 large egg whites, lightly beaten
1/4 cup Amaretto liqueur
1 teaspoon pure vanilla extract
3 large, ripe peaches, peeled, halved, and pitted

Preheat oven to 350 degrees.

In the workbowl of a food processor, combine almonds, confectioners' sugar, and superfine sugar. Operate the machine in short pulses until the nuts are very finely ground. With the machine off, add the lemon juice, egg whites, Amaretto, and vanilla extract. Pulse the machine in short bursts until the mixture becomes a smooth paste.

Remove almond mixture and divide it evenly among 6 individual shallow gratin dishes (or other small ovenproof plates), spreading it out on the plates. Place a peach half, cut side down, slightly off center in each dish. Press each peach half into almond mixture.

Bake in the center of the preheated oven until the almond mixture is well browned at outer edge and firm to the touch at the center, about 25 minutes. Remove from the oven and cool slightly.

To serve, place each dish on an underliner plate. Serve hot.

Cholesterol: 0 mg   Total Fat: 21 gm
Saturated Fat: 2 gm   Calories: 409

Home Cooking

Serves 6

Red Lentil Salad with Lardons
Turkey Roulade with White Wine Sauce
Scalloped Potatoes
Braised Fennel
Blueberry Pizzas

Red Lentil Salad with Lardons

This sensational first-course salad is a reinterpretation of one I remember from Postillion, a world-class restaurant in southern Germany. We kept the greens, the al dente little lentils, and the pleasing vinaigrette. But the generous sprinkling of lardons — chubby cubes of sautéed slab bacon — had to go. Still, the dish needed some smoke and a toothier texture. Turkey bacon provides both without putting your heart on red alert.

1 cup red lentils
Pinch of salt
1 cup Chicken Stock (see page 235)
1 large sweet red pepper, skin removed with a vegetable peeler, seeded
1 large sweet yellow pepper, prepared in the same as red pepper
1½ tablespoons balsamic vinegar
1 large shallot, peeled and finely chopped
3 tablespoons extra-virgin olive oil
1 tablespoon walnut oil
Salt
Freshly ground black pepper
¾ pound of mixed young salad greens, washed and dried
12 strips turkey bacon, cooked, drained, and crumbled into pieces

Soak lentils overnight in water to cover. The next day, drain them and discard soaking liquid.

Combine lentils, a pinch of salt, and the Chicken Stock in a pot and bring slowly to a simmer, stirring often. (Do not allow liquid to boil or the lentils will change color.) Simmer until just tender, 20–30 minutes. Strain, discard stock, and set aside.

Meanwhile, cut the red and yellow peppers into tiny cubes and set aside.

Prepare a vinaigrette by whisking together the vinegar, shallots, and olive and walnut oils. Add salt and pepper to taste.

Marinate the reserved lentils for about 1 hour in three-quarters of the vinaigrette.

To serve, toss the greens and pepper cubes in the remaining vinaigrette.

Divide among 6 salad plates. Evenly distribute the lentils in mounds in the middle of the greens. Garnish with the crumbled turkey bacon.

Cholesterol: 31 mg   Total Fat: 7 gm
Saturated Fat: 1 gm   Calories: 245

Turkey Roulade with White Wine Sauce

This dish is derived from one we used to do all the time. It seemed that whenever we catered a meal for a mayor, governor, or business tycoon, stuffed capon was the chosen entrée. Many people weren't eating red meat, and you could always count on someone not liking fish. It couldn't be duck ("too rich") or chicken ("too ordinary"), so capon it was. We stuffed it with a savory filling, and it was always a hit.

Here we eliminate the meat and cream from that stuffing, roll this less fatty version in a turkey breast instead, and end up with a tasty dish to set before a king.

1 double breast of turkey (2³/₄ pounds), boned, with skin intact

For the stuffing:

4 ounces fresh spinach, washed, blanched, chopped, and wrung out in cheesecloth to remove excess moisture
¹/₄ cup chopped watercress
2 teaspoons finely chopped fresh parsley
1 small shallot, peeled and finely chopped
1 tablespoon extra-virgin olive oil
2 tablespoons bread crumbs (made from cholesterol-free bread)
1 large egg white
¹/₈ teaspoon cayenne pepper
¹/₈ teaspoon freshly grated nutmeg
Salt
Freshly ground black pepper

For roasting the turkey breast:

1 small celery rib, coarsely chopped
1 large carrot, peeled and coarsely chopped
1 small onion, peeled and coarsely chopped

For the sauce:

1 cup dry white vermouth
4 cups Brown Chicken Stock (see page 235)
1 teaspoon arrowroot, dissolved in 1 tablespoon water
Salt
Freshly ground black pepper

Preheat oven to 350 degrees.

Being careful not to slice into the meat or puncture the skin, use a small, sharp knife to separate the tenderloins — a narrow strip of flesh on the underside of the breast — from the rest of the breast and set aside. Lay turkey breast between two sheets of plastic wrap, on a wooden board. Using a meat pounder, flatten the thicker part of the turkey breast to make it a uniform thickness. Keep the turkey breast wrapped in plastic and refrigerate until stuffing is made.

To make the stuffing, remove and discard the white tendon that runs the length of each turkey tenderloin. Cut the tenderloins into small chunks and place them in the workbowl of a food processor.

Add the spinach, watercress, parsley, shallot, olive oil, bread crumbs, and egg white to the workbowl. Operate the machine in short pulses until the contents are finely ground and well combined.

Add the cayenne pepper, nutmeg, and salt and pepper to taste. Pulse machine only enough to incorporate spices. Set aside.

Remove the turkey breast from the refrigerator and unwrap it. Place turkey, skin side down, on work surface. Remove stuffing mixture from the food processor and spread it evenly over one side of the turkey breast. Fold the other half of the breast over the stuffing.

Using metal skewers or wooden toothpicks, fasten the skin flaps along both sides of the breast together so that the stuffing is completely enclosed. There should be enough skin to completely cover the breast. Use a toothpick or skewer to fasten any loose skin at either end of breast. Set turkey breast aside.

Place the chopped celery, carrot, and onion in a roasting pan measuring approximately 13 x 9 x 2½ inches. Put the stuffed turkey breast on top of the vegetables.

Place the roasting pan in the center of the preheated oven and roast for 1 hour. Remove the pan from the oven and take out all the vegetables with a slotted spoon, leaving in the pan the fat that has collected from the turkey skin. Return the roasting pan to the oven and continue baking at 350 degrees for 1 hour more, or until the turkey reaches an internal temperature of 140 degrees.

Meanwhile, make the white wine sauce by combining the vegetables removed from the roasting pan with the vermouth and chicken stock, in a large, deep skillet (10–12 inches in diameter). Simmer over medium heat until liquid is reduced to ¾ cup, about 45 minutes. Remove from heat.

Pass through a sieve, discarding solids. Combine the strained liquid with the dissolved arrowroot in a very small saucepan (about 2-cup capacity). Stir constantly over medium heat until liquid thickens and just begins to boil, 3–4 minutes. Add salt and pepper to taste. Turn off heat until ready to serve.

To serve, remove turkey from oven and let rest in a warm place for 5 minutes. Remove the skewers, then remove and discard turkey skin. Using a very sharp slicing knife, cut two ¼-inch slices per person. If a skin has formed on the sauce, remove it. Reheat sauce quickly over high heat (do not let it boil) and spoon over turkey.

Note: The turkey breast can be stuffed and kept overnight in the refrigerator, well sealed with plastic wrap, before roasting.

Cholesterol: 91 mg   Total Fat: 5 gm
Saturated Fat: 1 gm   Calories: 266

Scalloped Potatoes

My friend Laurie Colwin is pure poetry when she describes what she made for supper the night before. She spends the majority of her time in a magical kitchen, smack in the middle of New York City, but a dead ringer for the heart of Vermont. She does everything by hand, and all of her dishes, pots, and pans come from a local flea market. This recipe started from one of hers. She brings these potatoes steaming to her huge wooden table in one of her extraordinary fifty-cent finds. Her guests take one look and swear, "Oh, I can't eat that!" She insists they can, and they do, and they're never sorry. Hers is made with 2 percent milk, ours with skim. We've also added some shiitake mushrooms and fresh thyme, although for straight comfort food you don't have to.

1 tablespoon canola (or other vegetable) oil, plus additional oil for
    greasing casserole dish
2 cloves garlic, peeled and finely chopped
4 ounces fresh shiitake mushrooms, stemmed and thinly sliced
1½ pounds russet potatoes, peeled and sliced paper-thin
Salt
Freshly ground black pepper
1½ teaspoons fresh thyme (or 1 teaspoon dried thyme)
1 cup evaporated skim milk
1 cup skim milk

Preheat oven to 350 degrees.

Heat oil in a nonstick skillet over medium heat. Add garlic and sauté 2 minutes. Stir in mushrooms and cook until soft, 5–6 minutes.

Lightly oil a 2-quart casserole dish. Layer a quarter of the potatoes on bottom of dish. Add salt and pepper. Sprinkle with a bit of the thyme and some of the mushroom-garlic mixture. Continue to layer all ingredients in this manner, finishing with a layer of potatoes.

Stir together the two milks and pour over potatoes.

Cover casserole with aluminum foil and place in preheated oven. Bake 30 minutes. Uncover and continue baking 30–40 minutes longer, until liquid is absorbed and potatoes are soft and browned on top.

Cholesterol: 2 mg   Total Fat: 3 gm
Saturated Fat: 0 gm   Calories: 179

Braised Fennel

I told you about Grilled Fennel in the previous menu. Now here's another way to serve this glorious vegetable, which I could eat every night of the week. In the braising the strong anise flavor is transformed into a subtle hint of its former self, while at the same time the texture changes from crunch to velvet. If you've never tasted this vegetable warm, you're in for a real treat.

1 tablespoon extra-virgin olive oil
1 large shallot, peeled and finely chopped
2 large fennel bulbs, stalks removed and bulbs cut lengthwise into 6
    wedges
2 tablespoons Pernod
2 cups Chicken Stock (see page 235)
Salt
Freshly ground black pepper

Heat oil in a large saucepan (about 4-quart capacity) over medium flame.

Add shallot and fennel. Cook until fennel is slightly browned on all sides, about 10 minutes.

Add Pernod and Chicken Stock. Allow liquid to just reach a boil, then reduce heat, cover pan, and simmer slowly until fennel is very tender, about 30 minutes. Uncover pot and remove fennel to a plate. Set aside.

Raise heat under saucepan in order to bring braising liquid to a boil. Allow liquid to boil, uncovered, until it is reduced by two-thirds.

Just before serving, return fennel to pan with boiling liquid. Cook, uncovered, until fennel is heated through, about 5 minutes. Season with salt and pepper to taste.

To serve, place two pieces of fennel on each plate. Spoon some of the poaching liquid over the top.

Note: Fennel may be braised several hours in advance of being reheated in its braising liquid.

Cholesterol: 2 mg   Total Fat: 3 gm
Saturated Fat: 0 gm   Calories: 46

Blueberry Pizzas

A guilt-free pizza is hard to come by, a pizzaless existence even harder. For those of you attempting to make the transition to life after pizza, this one's for you: a dessert pie so pleasing you won't even miss the mozzarella. Still feeling nostalgic for a slice of the old savory? Use this dough recipe, your favorite tomato sauce, and some fresh herbs.

2 cups blueberries, washed
$\frac{1}{4}$ cup granulated sugar

For the dough:

2 cups all-purpose flour, plus flour for preparing kneading surface
$\frac{1}{2}$ ounce (2 packages) active dry yeast
1 tablespoon granulated sugar, plus sugar to sprinkle on the crust
2 teaspoons fresh rosemary leaves
$\frac{1}{2}$ teaspoon salt
2 tablespoons extra-virgin olive oil, plus oil for greasing sheet pan
$\frac{3}{4}$ cup hot tap water (not to exceed 100 degrees)

In a bowl large enough to hold the blueberries, combine fruit and $\frac{1}{4}$ cup sugar. Set aside.

In the workbowl of a food processor, combine flour, yeast, 1 tablespoon sugar, rosemary, and salt. With steel blade in motion, pour oil and hot water through feed tube in a thin, steady stream. Process only until dough forms a ball around the center post of the machine.

Turn the dough onto a smooth, lightly floured surface and knead for 1 minute. Divide the dough into 6 equal balls. Flatten each with your hand. Using a rolling pin, form each ball into a 4-inch circle approximately $\frac{1}{4}$ inch thick. Transfer to a lightly oiled sheet pan. Using your fingers, create a raised rim around the perimeter of each circle.

Evenly distribute the fruit among the 6 pies. Sprinkle some granulated sugar evenly on each rim. Cover with a clean cloth towel and allow dough to rise for 1 hour.

Preheat oven to 400 degrees.

Bake pies in preheated oven for 25 minutes. Edges should be light brown. Cool before serving.

Note: The pizzas are best eaten shortly after baking. However, they may be held unwrapped at room temperature for several hours. If the pizzas are to be kept until the next day, wrap tightly and refrigerate. It will be necessary to reheat them somewhat to keep the crust tender.

Cholesterol: 0 mg	Total Fat: 4 gm
Saturated Fat: 1 gm	Calories: 263

Best of Bistro

Serves 6

Jicama and Butternut Squash with Warm Walnut Glaze
Cassoulet
Frisee, Red Radish, and Dandelion Salad
Open Orange Tart

Jicama and Butternut Squash
with Warm Walnut Glaze

Even a caterer sometimes has a cupboard resembling Mother Hubbard's — bare, that is. And it was on just such an evening that the idea for what has become one of our most requested starters was born. My family and I were eating giant rounds of kohlrabi (a little-known broccoli taste-alike that looks like a green baseball) with a bit of leftover vinaigrette, since that's all we had. Then the inspiration hit us: We could make something similar using a winter squash instead, add another vegetable, and sprinkle on a little crunch for a great first course. I mentioned the idea to Greg, who had some jicama lying around in his refrigerator. And the rest is history.

1 small jicama, cut into twelve $^{1}/_{4}$-inch slices
1 medium butternut squash, neck portion, cut into twelve $^{1}/_{4}$-inch slices
5 tablespoons walnut oil
1 tablespoon balsamic vinegar
1 tablespoon finely chopped walnuts, toasted
$^{1}/_{4}$ teaspoon granulated sugar
Salt
Freshly ground black pepper

In separate batches in a small, straight-sided pan, simmer the jicama and butternut squash in 2 inches of water until fork tender, 3–4 minutes. Use a slotted spoon to transfer the cooked vegetables from the water.

When cool enough to handle, use a cookie cutter to cut each piece into a 3-inch round. Reserve the rounds. Discard the trimmings or use in another recipe.

Make walnut dressing by adding the walnut oil, balsamic vinegar, chopped walnuts, and sugar to a small bowl. Stir with a whisk to combine. Add salt and pepper to taste. Set aside.

Using 2 slices of each vegetable, make a circle of the jicama and butternut squash on each of 6 first-course plates. Alternate and overlap the slices, keeping them close together, to create a pinwheel effect.

To serve, heat the walnut dressing in a small saucepan over medium flame until very hot, 3–4 minutes. Remove from heat and drizzle an equal amount of dressing over each serving.

Serve immediately.

Cholesterol: 0 mg   Total Fat: 12 gm
Saturated Fat: 2 gm   Calories: 135

Cassoulet

What is cassoulet? It's a meat and bean dish hailing from France's southwest. The beans are white, the meat is a combination of pork, sausages, lamb, preserved duck, all of it slowly cooked in goose fat. For many of us, this is truly a dish to die for — or from. Until now, that is. We present our version of cassoulet.

1/4 cup plus 2 teaspoons extra-virgin olive oil
1/2 pound turkey bacon (about 10 strips), roughly chopped
Two 2 1/2-pound rabbits, cut into pieces, seasoned with salt and pepper
2 large onions, peeled and diced
4 large garlic cloves, peeled and minced
2 large carrots, peeled and diced
7 cups dry white vermouth
4 cups Beef Stock (see page 234)
6 ounces tomato paste
2 teaspoons dried thyme
1/8 teaspoon ground cloves
4 bay leaves
1 pound Great Northern (or other dried white) beans, soaked overnight in
    enough water to cover, then drained
Salt
Freshly ground black pepper
2 cups white bread crumbs, made from stale cholesterol-free bread
1/2 cup finely chopped fresh parsley

In a large, low-sided, flameproof casserole heat 2 teaspoons of the olive oil over medium flame. Add turkey bacon and cook, stirring occasionally, until browned and crisp, about 5 minutes. Using a slotted spoon, remove bacon to a small bowl and set aside.

Using the same pot, add remaining 1/4 cup olive oil. Keeping heat at medium, add the rabbit, a few pieces at a time, sautéing until all pieces are browned, about 5 minutes on each side. When rabbit is browned, remove from pot and reserve.

Continuing to use the same pot, add onions, garlic, and carrots and cook over medium heat, stirring occasionally, until onions are translucent, 10–15 minutes.

Meanwhile, preheat oven to 350 degrees.

Add vermouth to the casserole and stir to loosen any browned particles from the bottom. Allow mixture to simmer 3–4 minutes, then pour in Beef Stock and raise heat to high. As soon as liquid reaches a boil, reduce heat and stir in the tomato paste, thyme, cloves, bay leaves, drained beans, and turkey bacon. Add rabbit, pressing the pieces into the liquid. Simmer for an additional 5 minutes.

Cover pot with ovenproof lid or aluminum foil and place in the center of the preheated oven. Bake covered for 2 hours without stirring. Remove cover and continue to cook with out stirring until beans are just tender and liquid has been absorbed, about 30 minutes more. Remove casserole from oven and cool to room temperature. Cover tightly with plastic wrap and refrigerate overnight to allow the flavors to blend and develop.

One hour before serving, remove cassoulet from refrigerator and discard plastic wrap. Remove and discard bay leaves. Place pot over medium heat and bring to a simmer. (This will take approximately 15 minutes.)

Meanwhile, preheat oven to 350 degrees.

Taste cassoulet for salt and pepper and correct the seasoning if necessary. Mix together bread crumbs and parsley. Sprinkle evenly over top of cassoulet.

Place pot in center of preheated oven. Bake until heated through, about 45 minutes, pressing down the browned crust every 15 minutes. Leave the final crust intact.

Remove from oven and allow to stand uncovered about 5 minutes, to cool slightly, before serving. Present the Cassoulet in an attractive casserole and serve at the table, or spoon onto individual warmed plates in the kitchen.

Cholesterol: 118 mg   Total Fat: 24 gm
Saturated Fat: 5 gm   Calories: 965

Frisee, Red Radish, and Dandelion Salad

Frisee is a salad green that resembles chicory, although it is more delicate and considerably less bitter. I used to order it in French bistros, where it was a classical accompaniment to cubes of bacon and croutons sautéed in butter. I don't anymore. But I missed its interesting flavor and lacy appearance. Here it is, without its fatty friends, served with tangy radish slices. We top it off with a salad dressing that gets its taste from sherry vinegar, an excellent staple to have in your pantry for an unusual and interesting vinaigrette.

Serve this salad as a separate course, after the Cassoulet.

1 pound dandelion greens, washed and dried, tough stems removed
2 large bunches red radishes, trimmed of stems, leaves, and tap root,
    washed and dried
1/2 pound frisee, individual leaves removed from head, washed, and dried
3 tablespoons Sherry Dressing (see below)

Break the dandelion leaves into 4-inch lengths. Slice the radishes into very thin rounds. (May be done ahead to this point.)

Just before serving, toss the dandelion with 1 tablespoon of the Sherry Dressing in a large bowl. Arrange a nest of dandelion greens nearly covering the surface of each of 6 chilled salad plates.

In the same bowl, toss the frisee with another tablespoon of the dressing, shaking off any excess dressing. Place a lightly packed mound of frisee at the center of each plate of dandelion.

Still using the same bowl, add the sliced radishes with the final tablespoon of dressing and toss. Cascade the radish slices over the frisee.

Cholesterol: 0 mg   Total Fat: 0 gm
Saturated Fat: 0 gm   Calories: 52

SHERRY DRESSING

1 small shallot, peeled and finely chopped
1 teaspoon Dijon mustard
4 tablespoons sherry wine vinegar

4 tablespoons canola (or other vegetable) oil

2 tablespoons extra-virgin olive oil

Salt

Freshly ground black pepper

In a small bowl combine the shallot, mustard, and vinegar. Stir with a whisk to combine.

Add the canola and olive oil in a slow, thin stream, whisking continuously. When the oils are incorporated, season with salt and pepper.

Yield: ⅔ cup

Note: Dressing will keep 3–5 days in the refrigerator in an airtight container.

1 tablespoon
Cholesterol: 0 mg   Total Fat: 7 gm
Saturated Fat: 1 gm   Calories: 64

Open Orange Tart

This fabulous tart is as gorgeous as it is delicious. The "frangipane" that lines its gossamer crust is a dead ringer for the real thing, which, up until this recipe, has always been made with eggs and butter. And the candied orange slices that sit on top suit it perfectly. The fruit must be made the night before, but it's easy. Should you have time, make extra. Just drain the orange slices, coat them with granulated sugar, and keep them to serve alongside a cup of espresso. If you can bear to part with them, they make for a great gift.

2 small navel oranges, sliced in ⅛-inch rounds, ends discarded

2 cups water, plus water for blanching oranges

1 cup granulated sugar

2 tablespoons orange liqueur

1 recipe Sweet Pastry Dough (see below)

1 recipe Frangipane Tart Filling (see below)

¼ cup apricot jam

2 tablespoons brandy (sugar syrup from oranges may be substituted)

Place orange slices in a large, low-sided pot (about 11-inch diameter). Add 2 inches of cold water. Place over medium heat. Bring just to a boil. Turn off heat and let stand 2 minutes. Drain oranges and repeat this process two more times. (Be careful not to boil the oranges or they will fall apart.) Drain oranges and set aside.

Rinse the pan well. Add 2 cups water and the sugar. Place over high heat and stir until sugar dissolves, about 2 minutes. Stop stirring and allow mixture to boil 5 minutes. Turn off heat.

Add the orange liqueur and stir to combine. Add the oranges. Lightly press them into the sugar syrup until they are submerged. Cover the pot with its lid and let stand overnight.

Drain the oranges and save the syrup for another purpose. Lay the slices on a double layer of paper towels to dry. Set aside.

Meanwhile, preheat oven to 375 degrees.

Line an 8½-inch tart pan with Sweet Pastry Dough as directed in recipe below. Place a sheet of foil over dough, covering the bottom and sides. Fill the foil-lined shell with pie weights (dried beans or rice can be substituted). Bake in the preheated oven for 10 minutes. Remove foil and weights and bake until bottom of pastry is golden, about 10 minutes more. Remove from oven. Lower oven temperature to 350 degrees. Cool crust slightly.

Spread Frangipane Tart Filling evenly over bottom of crust. Return tart to oven and bake until frangipane is set and turns opaque, about 15 minutes. Remove from oven.

When cool, arrange orange slices over the filling, overlapping them in a concentric circle around the outer edge of the tart. Repeat in center of tart to cover entire surface of frangipane. Set aside.

Heat the apricot jam with the brandy (or sugar syrup) until the mixture boils. Strain jam to remove any chunks of fruit. Brush the jam lightly over the oranges.

To serve, remove the tart from the pan and place it on a serving tray. Cut and serve at table.

Cholesterol: 0 mg   Total Fat: 19 gm
Saturated Fat: 2 gm   Calories: 357

SWEET PASTRY DOUGH

1 cup all-purpose flour
2 tablespoons granulated sugar
½ teaspoon salt

5 tablespoons canola (or other vegetable) oil

2 tablespoons plain nonfat yogurt

In a medium-size bowl, combine flour, sugar, and salt. Stir with a whisk to combine. Make a well in the center of this mixture. Add the oil and yogurt and stir together. Quickly work the dry ingredients into the liquid just until the mixture forms a ball. Wrap the dough in plastic. Refrigerate 1 hour.

Remove dough from refrigerator and place between two sheets of wax paper. Roll dough into a circle ¼–⅛ inch thick and about 10 inches in diameter. Remove top layer of wax paper.

Invert dough into a tart pan with a removable bottom. Press dough into place, then remove wax paper. Trim any excess dough from sides of pan.

Refrigerate dough-lined pan until ready to use.

Full recipe of dough
Cholesterol: 0 mg   Total Fat: 66 gm
Saturated Fat: 6 gm   Calories: 1,188

FRANGIPANE TART FILLING

¼ cup confectioners' sugar

¼ cup superfine sugar

½ cup blanched almonds

1 tablespoon all-purpose flour

2 teaspoons freshly squeezed lemon juice, strained

1 large egg white, lightly beaten

Combine the sugars, almonds, and flour in the workbowl of a food processor. Pulse in short bursts until nuts are finely ground.

With the motor running, add the lemon juice and egg white. Turn off machine when mixture becomes a paste, after about 30 seconds. Remove contents of workbowl to a container. Cover with an airtight lid.

Store in refrigerator.

Yield: About ¾ cup

Note: Frangipane will keep for about 10 days in refrigerator.

Full recipe of filling
Cholesterol: 0 mg   Total Fat: 48 gm
Saturated Fat: 5 gm   Calories: 804

A Milanese Menu

Serves 6

Wild Mushroom Sauté
Turkey Osso Buco
Risotto alla Milanese
Spinach with Garlic
Polenta Pound Cake
Plum Sauce

Wild Mushroom Sauté

The recipe we give you here is just an example of what you can do with this savory and flexible starter. Substitute any mushrooms you can find, prefer, or can afford. Use a bed of mixed greens instead of the radicchio, or even a giant slice of toasted bread. Stick with fresh herbs if you can, but they needn't be these, and in a pinch, dried will do. We usually serve this sauté warm, but room temperature works just fine, which would allow you to complete this course in advance if you like.

2 ounces dried porcini mushrooms
2 pounds fresh mushrooms, such as shiitake, portobello, or crimini
3 tablespoons extra-virgin olive oil
2 medium shallots, peeled and chopped
2 small garlic cloves, peeled and chopped
1 sprig fresh thyme
1 sprig fresh rosemary
Salt
Freshly ground black pepper
2 small heads radicchio, carefully separated into individual leaves, washed,
    and dried
2 tablespoons chopped fresh parsley

Soak the dried porcini in 1½ cups lukewarm water for at least 1 hour. Remove from water and rinse thoroughly in running water to remove dirt. Pour soaking liquid through a sieve lined with a paper towel or through a paper coffee filter to remove grit, and reserve.

Clean the fresh mushrooms with a soft brush or damp towel. Dry thoroughly. Discard stems (or save them for another purpose) and slice caps in ½-inch pieces. Set aside.

In a large frying pan, heat the olive oil over medium heat and sauté the shallots and garlic for 1–2 minutes. Add all the mushrooms, ½ cup of the liquid from the porcini, the thyme, and the rosemary. Cook until all the liquid has evaporated, stirring occasionally. Remove thyme and rosemary. Add salt and pepper to taste.

To serve, arrange several radicchio leaves on each of 6 small plates. Distribute the mushrooms among the plates, mounding them on the radicchio. Garnish with a sprinkle of chopped parsley.

Cholesterol: 0 mg   Total Fat: 7 gm
Saturated Fat: 1 gm   Calories: 123

Turkey Osso Buco

What a great pair of legs — turkey, that is! They are endlessly versatile in allowing us to capture the look and taste of a traditional dish, without the fat and cholesterol. Take this one, for example. Osso buco is usually made by braising veal shanks. But I defy you to tell the difference between that version and our own. In fact, unsuspecting guests have told us they have never had a better osso buco, even in Italy.

Spoon up this satisfying stew on individual plates accompanied by a mound of risotto and some garlicky greens (see following recipes), or take it to the table on a warm platter and serve family-style.

6 turkey drumsticks, skinned
Flour for dredging
1/4 cup extra-virgin olive oil
1 large onion, peeled and thinly sliced (about 1 cup)
1 bay leaf
1 carrot, peeled and chopped
1 celery rib, chopped
1/2 cup dry vermouth
One 28-ounce can imported crushed plum tomatoes
2 tablespoons chopped fresh parsley
1 large clove garlic, peeled and finely chopped
Zest of 1 lemon, finely grated
Salt
Freshly ground black pepper

Using a cleaver or large knife, remove the joint bone at the narrow end of each turkey drumstick. Cut each leg in half, perpendicular to the bone. Dredge each piece with flour.

Heat the olive oil in a large skillet. Add the turkey pieces and brown on all sides. Remove from pan and set aside. Add onions, bay leaf, carrot, and celery to the skillet and cook over medium heat approximately 5 minutes.

Pour in the vermouth and simmer until liquid has almost evaporated, about 10 minutes.

Add turkey pieces and tomatoes. Cover and simmer gently until tender, about 2 hours. (If necessary, add a small amount of additional vermouth during cooking to keep moist).

Remove turkey from skillet and set aside. Strain the sauce, discarding solids, and return remaining liquid along with turkey pieces to the pan. Stir in parsley, garlic, lemon zest, salt, and pepper. Simmer 5 minutes longer.

Serve turkey topped with sauce.

Cholesterol: 89 mg   Total Fat: 15 gm
Saturated Fat: 3 gm   Calories: 318

Risotto alla Milanese

This famous rice dish is the standard accompaniment to osso buco. Ours is different from the original since it is made with a splash of red wine and without butter, and we sprinkle on the Parmesan cheese just before serving. It is the same in its texture and distinctive saffron flavor. Form any leftovers into little cakes, chill until firm, and lightly sauté them in some extra-virgin olive oil. Serve them as an hors d'oeuvre or an unusual side dish.

2 tablespoons extra-virgin olive oil
1 small garlic clove, peeled and minced
1 small onion, peeled and finely chopped
1/4 cup dry Marsala (or red wine)
1 1/4 cups Arborio rice

5 cups boiling chicken stock, preferably homemade (see page 235), in
    which 10 strands of saffron have been dissolved
Salt
Freshly ground black pepper
Parmesan cheese, freshly grated

Heat the oil in a medium saucepan over medium heat. Sauté garlic and onion
until they become translucent, about 5 minutes. Add the Marsala and simmer
until the wine has evaporated and no liquid remains.

Stir in the rice, coating each grain with the oil-onion-garlic mixture, and
allowing it to heat through, about 3 minutes.

Maintaining medium heat, add 1 cup of the boiling saffron-infused chicken
stock to the rice mixture, stirring constantly until the rice has absorbed all the
liquid. Repeat this process until all the stock has been added and absorbed. The
rice should be slightly chewy and have a porridgelike consistency.

Add salt and pepper to taste.

Sprinkle each portion with a bit of Parmesan cheese before serving.

Cholesterol: 2 mg   Total Fat: 7 gm
Saturated Fat: 1 gm   Calories: 234

Spinach with Garlic

This punchy side dish holds its own against the forceful flavors of the osso buco
and its risotto. Be sure to wash the spinach carefully. A little sandy residue goes a
long way toward ruining the result.

4 tablespoons extra-virgin olive oil
3 large garlic cloves, peeled and slivered
3 pounds spinach, stemmed, washed, and dried
Salt
Freshly ground black pepper

Heat oil in a large casserole over medium heat. Add garlic slivers and reduce heat to low. Cook the garlic until it turns golden, being careful not to let it get too brown.

Add spinach and toss to coat with oil. Cover pot with lid and continue cooking over low heat until spinach is tender, about 10 minutes, stirring occasionally.

Turn off heat and keep spinach covered in pot until ready to serve.

Cholesterol: 0 mg   Total Fat: 7 gm
Saturated Fat: 1 gm   Calories: 124

Polenta Pound Cake

This simple and homey dessert was inspired by one that is currently knocking them dead (and could, with its fat and cholesterol content) at one of New York's chicest Italian restaurants. The polenta (cornmeal to us) adds an unusual rustic texture and gives this cake the body it needs to support its sauce of stewed plums. Hide a piece. It'll be great the following morning instead of your usual toast.

Solid vegetable shortening for preparing pan
1 cup Italian cornmeal for polenta, plus additional cornmeal to coat baking
    pan
1½ cups all-purpose flour
2 cups confectioners' sugar
1 teaspoon baking powder
½ teaspoon baking soda
½ cup unblanched whole almonds, finely ground
4 large egg whites, at room temperature
¼ teaspoon salt
¾ cup evaporated skim milk
2 tablespoons instant nonfat dry milk
½ cup canola (or other vegetable) oil
1 teaspoon pure vanilla extract

Preheat oven to 350 degrees.

Grease a 10 x 4½ x 3-inch (8-cup capacity) loaf pan with solid vegetable shortening. Dust with cornmeal. Invert and tap to remove any excess cornmeal. Set aside.

Combine 1 cup cornmeal, flour, confectioners' sugar, baking powder, baking soda, and ground almonds in a large bowl and stir with a whisk to combine. Set aside.

Using a whisk or an electric beater, beat egg whites until foamy. Add salt and continue to whip until stiff peaks form. Set aside.

In a small bowl thoroughly combine skim and dry milk, oil, and vanilla extract. Make a well in the center of the dry ingredients and pour in the milk-and-oil mixture. Stir just to combine. Fold in egg whites in two additions. Pour batter into prepared loaf pan.

Bake in the center of the preheated oven until a toothpick inserted into the middle of the cake comes out clean, 60–65 minutes. (The cake will have a rich brown crust.)

Remove pan from oven and cool on a rack for 15 minutes. Remove cake from pan and continue cooling on rack until cake reaches room temperature.

Serve each slice topped with a generous spoonful of Plum Sauce (next recipe).

Yield: 10 servings

Note: Wrapped tightly with plastic wrap, this cake will keep 5 days at room temperature or a week in the refrigerator. For best flavor, bring it to room temperature before serving.

1 slice
Cholesterol: 1 mg   Total Fat: 17 gm
Saturated Fat: 1 gm   Calories: 367

Plum Sauce

When we finally got the Polenta Pound Cake the way we wanted it, we knew it needed a compote — a red fruit stew, to be exact. We went back to our test kitchen and found the right taste in those perfect little oval Italian plums. Their sweet-and-sourness, combined with a potpourri of winter spices and a little rum to warm things up, gave us just what we were looking for.

Three 3-inch cinnamon sticks
3 allspice berries
2 whole cloves
2 tablespoons dark brown sugar
4 tablespoons granulated sugar
2 tablespoons dark rum
$\frac{1}{4}$ cup water
$1\frac{1}{2}$ pounds sweet red plums, pitted and cut into eighths

Tie cinnamon sticks, allspice, and cloves in a piece of cheesecloth. Place in a medium saucepan with both sugars, rum, and water. Bring to a boil over medium heat and allow the mixture to boil 3–4 minutes. Add plums and simmer until very tender, about 30 minutes. Remove and discard the spices in cheesecloth.

Pour plum mixture into a container and cool to room temperature. Cover tightly with lid and refrigerate.

Bring to room temperature before serving.

Yield: Approximately 3 cups

Note: Plum sauce may be refrigerated for up to 2 weeks.

2 tablespoons

Cholesterol: 0 mg	Total Fat: 0 gm
Saturated Fat: 0 gm	Calories: 22

Christmas

Serves 6

Lobster Bisque

Saddle of Venison

Port Wine Sauce

Roasted Chestnuts

Mashed Potatoes with Truffle Confetti

Julienne Root Vegetable Salad

Chocolate-Walnut Soufflés

Lobster Bisque

If it's Christmas dinner it needs to be luxurious. And what better way to start than with this elegant soup. Traditionally it is made with butter and cream, but we get the same result without the excess fat and cholesterol. Lobster in any form is special-occasion food. And since the hefty lobster taste is accomplished with relatively little of that precious shellfish, it's a Christmas present for your pocketbook as well as your heart.

2 tablespoons canola (or other vegetable) oil
2 large lobster tails (8 ounces each), meat and shells roughly chopped
2 tablespoons all-purpose flour
9 cups Lobster Stock (see page 237)
1 teaspoon paprika
1½ cups Yogurt Cheese (see page 239)
¾ cup evaporated skim milk
Salt
1 lobster tail (8 ounces), cooked, shelled, and sliced into 6 medallions
Chervil leaves (optional)

Heat the oil in a large saucepan (4-quart capacity) over medium flame. Add the lobster meat and shells. Stirring occasionally, cook until shells are bright red, about 3 minutes.

Add flour and stir to combine. Add the stock and simmer until reduced by one-third, about 1½ hours.

Add paprika, Yogurt Cheese, and evaporated skim milk. Stir until well blended and simmer 10 minutes longer. Remove from heat and cool slightly.

In small batches, puree the bisque in a food processor or blender until homogenous. Strain the bisque through a fine sieve, back into the same saucepan.

Add salt to taste and reheat before serving.

To serve, divide bisque into 6 preheated soup plates. Float a medallion of lobster and a few chervil leaves, if you can find them, in the center of each serving.

Note: Bisque can be made 24 hours in advance and kept in refrigerator. Bring to a boil before serving.

Cholesterol: 107 mg   Total Fat: 9 gm
Saturated Fat: 2 gm   Calories: 284

Saddle of Venison

Not so long ago, venison was only available to hunters and passionate fans willing to take out a mortgage to pay for it. But thanks to a number of deer farms located throughout the United States and New Zealand, it's now available to everyone. A succulent red meat, low in both fat and cholesterol, it provides a wonderful alternative to the usual standing rib roast or Christmas ham. Present it on your best platter surrounded by Roasted Chestnuts on a Christmas table decorated with candles, pine, and holly.

6-to-7-pound saddle of venison, bone in
3 tablespoons extra-virgin olive oil
2 small garlic cloves, peeled and minced
Salt
Freshly ground black pepper

Preheat oven to 500 degrees.

Rub oil over entire surface of venison. Rub meat with garlic, salt, and pepper. Place meat, bone down, in a shallow baking dish.

Put dish in the center of the preheated oven and reduce heat to 350 degrees. Cook for 60–70 minutes, or until the desired internal temperature (135 degrees for rare, 145 degrees for medium, 155 degrees for well done) is reached.

Remove venison from oven and cover with aluminum foil. Let stand in a warm place for 10 minutes.

Carve meat away from each side of bone. Slice into ¼-inch-thick medallions and transfer to a warm serving platter.

To serve, spoon a small amount of hot Port Wine Sauce (see next recipe), along with any meat juices obtained when carving, over venison. Pass remaining sauce separately.

Serving includes 2 tablespoons Port Wine Sauce
Cholesterol: 125 mg   Total Fat: 16 gm
Saturated Fat: 5 gm   Calories: 350

Port Wine Sauce

A port wine sauce lends itself to venison since its sweetness offsets the gaminess of the meat. And its lush garnet color looks gorgeous on the plate. Bring plenty more to the table in a sauceboat. If your guests are anything like ours, there won't be a drop left.

8 cups Brown Chicken Stock (see page 235)
2 cups dry red wine
6 medium shallots, peeled and sliced
3 ounces port
Arrowroot, or other thickener
Salt
Freshly ground black pepper

In a saucepan, reduce chicken stock, red wine, and shallots to a quantity of 10 ounces (1¼ cups). Put through a sieve and discard solids. Add port and continue cooking a few minutes longer, reducing a bit more.

Dissolve arrowroot in a little red wine or water, and add a small amount to slightly thicken the sauce.

Add salt and pepper to taste.

Yield: 1½ cups

2 tablespoons
Cholesterol: 0 mg   Total Fat: 2 gm
Saturated Fat: 0.3 gm Calories: 76

Roasted Chestnuts

"Chestnuts roasting on an open fire" are the very image of Christmas. And open fire or not, they belong at the Christmas table. Choose firm, plump nuts that are free of shell blemishes. And get your friends and family to help lighten the tedious job of peeling them, over a glass of champagne or robust red wine.

1 pound fresh chestnuts, washed
2 tablespoons extra-virgin olive oil
1/4 cup Calvados
Salt
Freshly ground pepper

Preheat oven to 400 degrees.

Being careful not to cut into the meat of the chestnuts, cut an X through the shiny top of each shell. Place the chestnuts in one layer on a sheet pan and roast them in the preheated oven for 20 minutes.

Remove from oven. When just cool enough to handle, peel the chestnuts, removing the shell and the papery skin beneath. (Do not let them cool completely, for they are much easier to peel when warm.)

Just before serving, heat the oil in a sauté pan large enough to hold all the chestnuts in one layer. Stir-fry the nuts to a light brown. Transfer the chestnuts to paper toweling and blot off excess oil.

Degrease the pan. Deglaze the pan with Calvados. Over high heat, reduce the Calvados by one-half.

Return the chestnuts to the pan. Stir to glaze with the reduced Calvados. Season to taste with salt and pepper.

Cholesterol: 0 mg   Total Fat: 6 gm
Saturated Fat: 1 gm   Calories: 223

Mashed Potatoes with Truffle Confetti

These mashed potatoes are truly first-rate, and they don't have a drop of butter, milk, or cream. They can come to the Christmas party all by themselves, but should you want to splurge, add a confetti of truffles.

We got the idea from friend and four-star chef Jean-Georges Vongerichten of New York's JoJo's restaurant. His fame has come from a unique style of light cooking in which he uses innovative oil infusions, bouillons, and vinaigrettes. But for Christmas with friends, he returns to the holiday foods of his Alsatian childhood, serving a memorable goose stew that is accompanied by warm red cabbage and mashed potatoes peppered with truffles. Our low-fat version of his truffled potatoes offers its own sublime results.

1 small black truffle (optional)

2 pounds russet potatoes, scrubbed

¼ cup extra-virgin olive oil

2 teaspoons salt

¼ teaspoon freshly ground white pepper

¼ teaspoon freshly ground black pepper

¼ cup Chicken Stock (see page 235) or potato cooking liquid

Using a vegetable peeler, shave thin sheets from the truffle. With a sharp knife, chop the sheets into "confetti" bits. Reserve.

Peel potatoes and cut into large pieces. Immediately place them in a large pot and cover with cold water. Over high heat, bring to a full boil. Lower heat and simmer, covered, until potatoes are tender, about 25 minutes. Drain.

Return potatoes to the pot. Add olive oil, salt, white and black pepper, and Chicken Stock or cooking liquid. Mash to desired consistency.

Stir in truffle confetti. Serve immediately.

Note: Potatoes can be held in a lightly greased baking dish in a warm oven.

Cholesterol: 0 mg	Total Fat: 9 gm
Saturated Fat: 1 gm	Calories: 224

Julienne Root Vegetable Salad

This whole array of hearty winter vegetables, with their robust texture and subtle sweetness, makes an appearance all season long at our table. We fancy them up for the holiday by giving them a special cut and an elegant dressing.

With this menu, we like to serve the salad as a separate course. Like so much of this meal, the vegetables can be partially prepared ahead of time. Peel and cut them and hold in cold water until time to cook them.

Round up any leftover venison, cube it, and mix it with some more of this salad for an instant next-day lunch.

For the dressing:

¼ cup Mayonnaise (see page 238)
¼ cup plain nonfat yogurt
1 small shallot, peeled and very finely minced
¼ teaspoon finely minced garlic
1 tablespoon whole-grain mustard
2 tablespoons chopped fresh parsley
Salt
Freshly ground black pepper

For the vegetable julienne:

1 small celery root (celeriac), trimmed and peeled
1 small rutabaga, peeled
2 large carrots, trimmed and peeled
2 large parsnips, trimmed and peeled
½ pound red beets, trimmed and peeled

1 pound radicchio, leaves separated, washed, and dried

In a small bowl, combine Mayonnaise and yogurt. Stir in shallot, garlic, mustard, and parsley. Season to taste with salt and pepper. Reserve.

Cut all the root vegetables into batons about 1½ inches long and ⅛–¼ inch square.

In a large pot, bring a gallon of water to a rapid boil. In separate batches, starting with the celery root and ending with the beets, cook each vegetable for 1 minute. As each batch is cooked, use a wire strainer or slotted spoon to immediately transfer the vegetables to a bowl containing 1 quart of cold water and 1 pound of ice. Transfer that batch to paper toweling to dry, then proceed with cooking and cooling the next batch.

It is very important that you cook the red beets last, since they will discolor the cooking and refreshing liquids, and could discolor the other vegetables. Reserve the beets separately. They will be used as a garnish.

To serve, fashion a few radicchio leaves into a loose cup on each of 6 chilled salad plates. In a medium-size bowl, combine the celery root, rutabaga, carrots, and parsnips, and carefully toss them with 4 tablespoons of the dressing. Correct the seasoning. Place a loosely packed mound of dressed vegetables at the center of each cluster of radicchio leaves. Cascade the beets over the top.

Cholesterol: 0 mg   Total Fat: 6 gm
Saturated Fat: 1 gm   Calories: 98

Chocolate-Walnut Soufflés

Every caterer has his chocolate cake. Ours was a nearly flourless one, leaving more room for the eggs, butter, and chocolate. Its replacement began with one developed by Rozanne Gold for a spa restaurant. It was rich enough to seem as if it had gotten through the door by accident. As with most recipes, that one also started someplace else — Edda Servi Maclin's *Classic Cooking of the Italian Jews*. We transformed it into a soufflé for a chocolate extravaganza as heavenly as it is healthy.

6 large egg whites, at room temperature
1/2 teaspoon salt
1/3 cup unsweetened cocoa powder
3/4 cup granulated sugar, plus sugar for preparing ramekins
2 tablespoons canola (or other vegetable) oil, plus oil for preparing
    ramekins
1 teaspoon instant espresso powder dissolved in 1 tablespoon warm water
1 cup finely chopped walnuts

Preheat oven to 400 degrees.

In a large bowl, beat egg whites and salt together to achieve a stiff-peaked meringue. Set aside.

In a bowl large enough to hold the entire recipe, combine the cocoa powder and 3/4 cup sugar. Using a rubber spatula, work the 2 tablespoons oil and espresso powder into the cocoa mixture to form a stiff paste. Thoroughly mix in the walnuts and one-third of the beaten egg whites. Gently fold in the remaining egg whites.

Lightly oil and sugar six 1-cup soufflé ramekins. Divide the batter among the prepared ramekins. Place in the preheated oven and bake for about 20 minutes.

Serve immediately.

Note: Uncooked soufflés may be tightly covered and refrigerated for up to 4 hours.

Cholesterol: 0 mg   Total Fat: 21 gm
Saturated Fat: 3 gm   Calories: 342

SPRING

A Taste of the Orient —
A Brunch Buffet

Serves 6

Chinese Treasure Soup

Sweet and Sour Chicken

Alicia Chen's Chicken and String Bean Stir-Fry

Minnie Chin's Cabbage and Vermicelli

New Sesame Noodles

Vegetable Kebabs

Chinese Cabbage and Daikon Salad

Asian Fruit Fantasy

Chinese Treasure Soup

We launch this Asiatic brunch with a hot soup that is served at table. Beginning the meal with a sit-down course allows guests to get acquainted before they go off to forage for themselves at the buffet. It starts with a rich chicken stock, enhanced by a variety of characteristic Chinese flavors. Floating in the clear broth are some goodies that provide both texture and visual interest. If you're near a Chinatown, pick up some pretty porcelain soup bowls and spoons. They're a great investment — inexpensive and a marvelous table dresser-upper.

7 cups Chicken Stock (see page 235)
2 tablespoons finely grated peeled fresh ginger
3 small garlic cloves, peeled and crushed
2 tablespoons Oriental sesame oil
6 large dried shiitake mushrooms
24 snow peas, blanched and drained, trimmed of stems and strings
4 ounces soft tofu, cut into $1/4$-inch cubes
2 scallions, greens only, sliced on the bias $1/8$ inch thick

In a 4-quart saucepan combine Chicken Stock, ginger, garlic, sesame oil, and mushrooms. Place over medium-high heat and bring to a boil. Lower heat and simmer for 10 minutes. Remove from heat and pass through a fine sieve. Retrieve mushrooms. Discard all other solids remaining in sieve.

Return the liquid and mushrooms to the saucepan and bring to a boil over medium heat.

Meanwhile, in a wide, shallow pan with a tightly fitting lid, bring $1/2$ inch water to a boil. Add the snow peas. Cover and steam just until they have puffed, about 1 minute. Drain.

To serve, divide the tofu cubes, snow peas, and scallions evenly among 6 soup bowls. Ladle the hot soup and mushrooms into the bowls. Serve immediately.

Cholesterol: 0 mg   Total Fat: 8 gm
Saturated Fat: 1 gm   Calories: 126

Sweet and Sour Chicken

This incredibly easy dish is always a crowd pleaser. The chicken becomes so tender after hours of cooking (that's right, almost four) that we've seen guests even eat the bones. People like to pick up the pieces, so provide plenty of napkins. But don't be surprised if people lick up that sweet-spicy sauce with their fingers. Keep this recipe in mind for a great hors d'oeuvre as well, using the drumstick part of a chicken wing.

1/2 cup mild honey
1/2 cup light brown sugar
1/4 cup malt vinegar
1/2 cup soy sauce
6 large garlic cloves, peeled and minced
1/4 cup finely grated peeled fresh ginger
1/4 teaspoon hot red pepper flakes
4 chicken drumsticks, skin removed
4 chicken thighs, skin removed

Preheat oven to 325 degrees.

In a small bowl combine honey, brown sugar, and vinegar. Stir together until sugar dissolves. Add the soy sauce, garlic, ginger, and red pepper flakes. Stir until mixture is a smooth sauce. Set aside.

Place the chicken pieces in a baking dish about 12 x 9 x 2 inches. Pour the reserved mixture over the chicken. Turn each piece to coat with sauce. Cover dish tightly with aluminum foil.

Place in the center of the preheated oven and cook for 3 hours. Uncover the dish. Raise the temperature to 375 degrees. Turn the chicken parts and continue to bake, uncovered, until the chicken is tender and very brown. The sauce should have reduced by two-thirds. This should take an additional 45 minutes. Remove from oven.

To serve, transfer chicken to a warm serving tray. Pour the sauce over it. Serve hot.

1 piece chicken, with sauce
Cholesterol: 69 mg   Total Fat: 4 gm
Saturated Fat: 1 gm   Calories: 236

Alicia Chen's Chicken and String Bean Stir-Fry

I met Alicia Chen while doing a newspaper story on baby-sitters who are great cooks. She taught me four authentic Chinese dishes in a half hour without using a word of English. This quick and easy one was so addictive that I made it daily for weeks. Alicia used ground pork, but I substituted chicken with no change in outcome. You cannot, however, substitute for the barbecue sauce, an unusual, aromatic brew that gives this dish its unique flavor. Serve it, if you like, with steamed white rice.

3 tablespoons canola (or other vegetable) oil
2 small garlic cloves, peeled and minced
2 tablespoons Chinese barbecue sauce (available in Oriental food shops)
6 ounces ground chicken
$^3/_4$ pound string beans, cleaned, cut into thirds, boiled in salted water for 3
    minutes, and drained
Salt
$1^1/_2$ teaspoons cornstarch, dissolved in $^1/_4$ cup warm water
$1^1/_2$ tablespoons soy sauce

Heat oil in a wok or large nonstick frying pan (about 11-inch diameter) over medium flame. Add garlic and cook, stirring frequently, until it becomes golden, 2–3 minutes. Add the barbecue sauce and the chicken. Cook, stirring to break up the chicken, until the chicken becomes opaque, 4–5 minutes.

Add the string beans. Cover the pan with a lid and cook for 2 minutes, stirring occasionally.

Remove lid. Add salt to taste. Add cornstarch mixture and soy sauce. Stir and heat through until sauce begins to bubble and becomes translucent, 3–4 minutes.

Transfer to a warm platter and serve hot.

Cholesterol: 17 mg   Total Fat: 11 gm
Saturated Fat: 1 gm   Calories: 162

Minnie Chin's Cabbage and Vermicelli

Many of my most successful recipes come from unexpected sources. Take this one from Minnie Chin, a veritable Mary Poppins from Borneo who looks after a neighbor's children and is also a superb cook. I originally tracked her down from the mouth-watering aromas emanating from behind her door, and we have been cooking friends ever since. Before Minnie, I was convinced I could never duplicate an authentic Chinese taste. I was ready to turn in my wok until I tried this dish. Don't be discouraged if you can't find fried gluten. (What is it? Flour is composed of starch and protein. Gluten is the protein, and is sold fresh or canned in Oriental neighborhoods.) Just leave it out. No one will know the difference.

3 tablespoons peanut oil
2 small garlic cloves, peeled and minced
1 1/2 teaspoons finely grated peeled fresh ginger
1/2 small Chinese cabbage, shredded
2 small carrots, peeled and julienned
Three 3-ounce bags Chinese vermicelli noodles, soaked in warm water for
        10 minutes, drained
3/4 cup water
Salt
Two 6-ounce cans fried gluten (available in Oriental food shops)
Oriental sesame oil
Soy sauce

Heat oil in a wok or a deep nonstick frying pan (about 11-inch diameter) over medium-high flame. Add garlic and ginger. Cook, stirring frequently, until they are golden, 2–3 minutes.

Add cabbage and carrots. Continue cooking, stirring occasionally, until these vegetables are almost soft, about 5 minutes.

Add vermicelli, water, and salt to taste. Add entire contents of fried gluten cans. Heat through, 2–3 minutes.

Splash in a small amount of sesame oil and soy sauce to flavor.
Transfer to a warm serving platter and serve hot.

Cholesterol: 0 mg   Total Fat: 11 gm
Saturated Fat: 2 gm   Calories: 382

New Sesame Noodles

So what if sesame noodles are so commonplace that New York neighborhood Chinese restaurants throw them in with any order over ten dollars? People love them. We've been making them since we began catering, and they're still going strong. I must say that our version is a cut above the ordinary, since we add a number of unique ingredients that make for an unusual result. Remember to check the ingredients on the noodle package. No eggs, please.

1 tablespoon freshly squeezed lemon juice, strained
2 tablespoons peanut (or other vegetable) oil
1 large garlic clove, peeled and minced
1/4 cup tahini (a sesame paste available in Oriental and Middle Eastern food shops)
6 tablespoons smooth peanut butter
1 1/2 cups Chicken Stock (see page 235)
2 tablespoons soy sauce
4 teaspoons Oriental sesame oil
2 tablespoons dark brown sugar
8 ounces Chinese noodles or spaghetti, cooked, drained, and tossed with 1 tablespoon sesame oil
2 scallions, greens only, thinly sliced on the bias

Combine lemon juice, peanut oil, garlic, tahini, peanut butter, Chicken Stock, soy sauce, sesame oil, and brown sugar in a blender or food processor. Puree until all ingredients combine to form a smooth paste.

Place this paste and the cooked noodles in a large bowl. Toss to evenly coat noodles. Let stand 1 hour at room temperature. Retoss just before serving, to redistribute sauce. Garnish with scallions.

Cholesterol: 0 mg   Total Fat: 24 gm
Saturated Fat: 4 gm   Calories: 414

Vegetable Kebabs

Kebabs enhance any buffet. Here we serve them in a sweet and sour marinade that complements the other foods on the table. We like the lively color and crunch of the peppers, paired with the savory mushrooms. But other combinations work equally well, using the same technique.

2 tablespoons soy sauce
2 teaspoons Oriental sesame oil
1 small garlic clove, peeled and minced
1 teaspoon finely grated peeled fresh ginger
$1/8$ teaspoon hot red pepper flakes
1 tablespoon mild honey
1 large sweet red pepper, cored, seeded, and cut into 12 squares
1 large sweet yellow pepper, cored, seeded, and cut into 12 squares
12 small fresh shiitake mushrooms
6 fresh oyster mushrooms

Make a marinade by combining the soy sauce, sesame oil, garlic, ginger, red pepper flakes, and honey in a medium-size bowl. Stir until ingredients are well combined and honey dissolves.

Add the peppers and mushrooms. Toss to coat the vegetables with the marinade. Let stand at room temperature for 2 hours.

Thread the mushrooms and peppers onto 6 long wooden skewers. On each skewer begin with a square of red pepper, followed by a shiitake mushroom, then a square of yellow pepper, then an oyster mushroom. Continue with another square of red pepper and shiitake mushroom, and end with a piece of yellow pepper. (Save any remaining marinade and use with chicken, fish, or vegetables.)

Heat a ridged, nonstick grill pan over high heat until it begins to smoke, 2–3 minutes. Place the skewers on the pan and reduce heat to low. Cook until vegetables begin to brown and soften, about 5 minutes.

Turn kebabs and continue to grill until peppers are tender, about 5 minutes more.

Remove from grill pan and place on a warm serving tray. Serve hot.

Cholesterol: 0 mg   Total Fat: 1 gm
Saturated Fat: 0 gm   Calories: 39

Chinese Cabbage and Daikon Salad

Japanese flavors inspire this fresh-tasting salad. As a palate refresher after all those exotic dishes, this works perfectly. Chinese cabbage has become widely available in produce stores and supermarkets. But should you be unable to find daikon (a large Asian radish with a sweet, fresh taste), ordinary red radishes can be substituted. Leftover fresh daikon can be kept under refrigeration for a week, wrapped in plastic.

1 tablespoon finely grated peeled fresh ginger
2 teaspoons soy sauce
6 tablespoons mirin (available in Oriental food shops)
3 tablespoons sake
$1/4$ teaspoon granulated sugar
2 cups coarsely grated peeled daikon
4 cups shredded Chinese cabbage
1 large carrot, peeled and julienned

In a large bowl, combine ginger, soy sauce, mirin, sake, and sugar. Stir with a whisk until sugar dissolves.

Add the daikon, cabbage, and carrots. Toss until the salad is well coated with dressing.

Transfer to a salad bowl before serving.

Cholesterol: 0 mg   Total Fat: 0 gm
Saturated Fat: 1 gm   Calories: 46

Asian Fruit Fantasy

Our original idea for the dessert to serve with this buffet was a trifle — layers of fruit alternating with a custard in a beautiful stemmed glass bowl. After extensive experimentation we came up with one. It even passed the low-cholesterol test. But guests tended to ignore the custard and eat the fragrant tropical fruit. So an exotic fruit salad it became. There's an important lesson to be learned here. Complicated does not necessarily mean better. Don't be afraid to serve something simple; it often works best.

1 large papaya, peeled, seeded, and cubed
1 large mango, peeled, pitted, and cubed
3 kiwis, peeled, cut in quarters lengthwise, and cubed
24 litchi nuts, peeled, pitted, and halved (canned may be substituted)

Combine all the fruit in a large bowl. Toss together. Refrigerate 1 hour. Toss again. Transfer to a serving bowl.

Cholesterol: 0 mg   Total Fat: 0 gm
Saturated Fat: 0 gm   Calories: 80

Mediterranean Medley Lunch

Serves 6

Vegetable Paella
Escarole and Tomato Salad
Portuguese-Style Sweet Bread
Marinated Orange Balls
Pistachio Cookies

Vegetable Paella

Paella is a Spanish dish that takes its name from the pan in which it is cooked. In its traditional form, it combines saffron-flavored rice with an assortment of shellfish, poultry, and sausage. It is a wonderful meal for company, but alas, it is loaded with cholesterol. In our version, saffron, the main flavoring agent, remains to give the paella its characteristic taste and color, while the substitution of vegetables for the meat, fish, and chicken makes for something new, light, and healthy.

Bring it to the table with the salad and bread we have created to go with it, and dig in.

3 tablespoons extra-virgin olive oil
2 medium onions, peeled and diced
3 leeks, white part only, diced and washed thoroughly
3 large tomatoes, peeled, seeded, and diced
2 medium sweet red peppers, seeded and diced
1 medium sweet green pepper, seeded and diced
1 pint box small brussels sprouts, outer leaves removed
1 cup peas, fresh or frozen
10–12 threads saffron
1 cup dry white wine
3 large cloves of garlic, peeled and minced
¼ cup finely chopped fresh parsley
1 pound Arborio (or other short-grain) rice
6½ cups Chicken Stock (see page 235)
Juice of 1 lemon, strained
Salt
Freshly ground black pepper

In a large, heavy-bottomed casserole, heat oil over medium flame until hot. Add onions, leeks, and tomatoes. Simmer, stirring occasionally, until mixture is pastelike, about 10 minutes. Stir in peppers, brussels sprouts, peas, saffron, and wine. Bring to a boil. Reduce heat and simmer 10 more minutes, stirring once or twice.

Add garlic, parsley, rice, and Chicken Stock. Stir to combine. Cook over medium heat without stirring until rice is done and liquid has evaporated, 25–30 minutes.

Sprinkle with lemon juice. Fluff rice with a fork and add salt and pepper to taste.

Cholesterol: 0 mg	Total Fat: 4 gm
Saturated Fat: 0 gm	Calories: 463

Escarole and Tomato Salad

Escarole is a hearty green whose slightly bitter taste and fresh, crisp texture make it a good choice here. When combined with beefy wedges of tomato and a hint of onion, it makes a salad that stands up to its strong, tangy, bittersweet dressing.

2 small heads escarole, washed, dried, and torn into small pieces
2 medium ripe tomatoes, cut into thin wedges
1 small red onion, peeled and sliced into paper-thin rounds
$1/2$ cup Sun-Dried Tomato Vinaigrette (see below)
Salt
Freshly ground black pepper

Combine escarole, tomato wedges, and onion slices in a large bowl. Add Sun-Dried Tomato Vinaigrette and toss until salad is well coated. Add salt and pepper to taste.

To serve, distribute escarole salad equally among 6 chilled salad plates. Arrange a few onion rounds and tomato wedges on top.

Cholesterol: 0 mg	Total Fat: 14 gm
Saturated Fat: 2 gm	Calories: 147

SUN-DRIED TOMATO VINAIGRETTE

1 tablespoon sun-dried tomato puree
2 teaspoons tomato paste
$1/4$ teaspoon granulated sugar

1 tablespoon red wine vinegar
1 tablespoon balsamic vinegar
3 tablespoons extra-virgin olive oil
3 tablespoons canola (or other vegetable) oil
Salt
Freshly ground black pepper

In a small bowl combine sun-dried tomato puree, tomato paste, and sugar. Stir with a whisk to make a smooth paste. Add the red wine and balsamic vinegars. Continue stirring while slowly adding the olive and canola oils. When well blended add salt and pepper to taste.

Yield: About ½ cup

Note: This dressing will keep several weeks in the refrigerator in an airtight container.

1 tablespoon
Cholesterol: 0 mg   Total Fat: 10 gm
Saturated Fat: 1 gm   Calories: 90

Portuguese-Style Sweet Bread

I first tasted Portuguese sweet bread over twenty years ago. I was in a crowded automobile, coming home from a summer weekend in Massachusetts, on a hot, sticky day. All in all, it was a hideous trip, redeemed by the fact that we stopped in Rhode Island and someone bought this bread. I was sure its yellow color, cloudlike texture, and softly sweet taste could only have come from that unholy triumvirate, butter, whole milk, and eggs. We found a way to do without those ingredients and still come up with a wonderful loaf whose sweetness works with the strong, savory flavors of the other parts of this meal. Make a lot. It goes fast.

1 cup evaporated skim milk (warmed to 100–115 degrees)
2 packages active dry yeast
¾ cup plus 1 teaspoon granulated sugar
2 tablespoons instant nonfat dry milk

$^{1}/_{3}$ cup canola (or other vegetable) oil

4 large egg whites, beaten until foamy

1 tablespoon salt

4$^{1}/_{2}$ cups all-purpose flour, plus additional flour for dusting kneading
    surface

Vegetable oil for greasing bowl

Combine $^{1}/_{2}$ cup evaporated skim milk, yeast, and 1 teaspoon sugar. Stir to dissolve yeast. Allow mixture to proof about 10 minutes. Put the remaining $^{1}/_{2}$ cup evaporated skim milk, $^{3}/_{4}$ cup sugar, instant nonfat dry milk, and oil in a small bowl and mix well. Add this to the yeast mixture. Stir in the beaten egg whites and salt.

Add 4 cups of flour, a cup at a time. Using hands, knead in the bowl to make a soft, sticky dough.

Turn out onto a floured surface. Knead until the dough is smooth and elastic, about 10 minutes, using the remaining flour to keep dough from sticking. (The dough should remain very soft and slightly sticky.)

Shape dough into a ball and put into an oiled bowl, turning to coat entire surface. Cover bowl tightly with plastic wrap and let dough rise in a warm, draft-free place until it has doubled in bulk, about 1$^{1}/_{2}$ hours.

Punch down the dough and divide it in half. Shape each half into a ball and place it in a 9-inch nonstick, ovenproof skillet (or use lightly oiled cake pans). Cover the skillets with a damp towel and let the dough rise again until doubled in bulk, about 1 hour.

Meanwhile, preheat oven to 350 degrees. When dough has again risen, place the skillets in the oven and bake until the bread is dark brown and sounds hollow when tapped on top and bottom, about 40 minutes.

Remove loaves from skillets and cool on a rack before slicing.

Yield: 2 round loaves

Note: This bread will keep at room temperature, wrapped in plastic, for 2–3 days. It can also be frozen for several months, in which case it should be warmed in the oven before serving.

$^{1}/_{6}$ loaf
Cholesterol: 1 mg   Total Fat: 6 gm
Saturated Fat: 1 gm   Calories: 229

Marinated Orange Balls

This mouth-watering dessert, whose refreshing citrus taste works perfectly after the strong flavors of the salad and paella, begins working its magic the moment your guests lay eyes on it. Show off these glistening orange spheres by bringing them to the table in a large glass bowl before spooning into individual dishes. This dish can be made ahead — an important bonus for the cook.

7 cups water
4 cups granulated sugar
10 small navel oranges
1 cup Grand Marnier (or similar orange liqueur)
½ cup grenadine syrup

Make a sugar syrup by combining 6 cups of water with 3 cups of sugar in a large pot. Bring to a boil over high heat. Reduce heat and simmer 5 minutes. Remove pot from heat and set the syrup aside.

Using a vegetable peeler, remove zest from the oranges and cut it into thin strips. Set zest aside.

Peel oranges and remove as much of the white pith from each orange as possible. Place oranges in a large stockpot. Add the Grand Marnier and the sugar syrup. Over a high flame, heat until the syrup just begins to boil, then reduce heat and simmer 15 minutes.

Meanwhile, combine the remaining cup of water and cup of sugar with the grenadine syrup. Bring to a boil over medium heat and simmer for 5 minutes. Add the julienned orange zest and continue to simmer 5 more minutes. Using a strainer, remove zest and allow to drain. Discard the grenadine liquid.

When the oranges have simmered 15 minutes, carefully remove them from the liquid. Refrigerate in a single layer.

Allow sugar syrup to cool to room temperature. Refrigerate.

Serve individual oranges with some of the zest and some syrup.

1 orange, with 2 tablespoons syrup
Cholesterol: 0 mg   Total Fat: 0 gm
Saturated Fat: 0 gm   Calories: 140

Pistachio Cookies

Melanie Ress, a New York food consultant and former caterer, grew up in a home where fine food was made and appreciated. Her parents are gourmets who still enjoy keeping up with the New York restaurant scene. And her mother is famous for a question she asks at the end of every meal, no matter how rich or lavish. "Don't you have a little cookie?" We're with you, Mrs. Ress, and here it is.

2 large egg whites, at room temperature
6 tablespoons confectioners' sugar
¼ cup all-purpose flour
2 tablespoons canola (or other vegetable) oil, plus oil to grease cookie
    sheet
1 teaspoon pure vanilla extract
2 tablespoons finely chopped pistachio nuts

Preheat oven to 325 degrees.

Combine egg whites, sugar, flour, oil, and vanilla extract in a small bowl. Stir with a whisk to make a smooth, thin batter. Set aside.

Liberally grease a cookie sheet with oil.

Make four round pools of batter, 2 teaspoons each, evenly spaced on the cookie sheet. Sprinkle each pool with ¼ teaspoon pistachio nuts.

Place in the center of the oven and bake until the edges of the cookies are brown and the center begins to turn golden, about 8 minutes.

Remove pan from oven and loosen cookies with a metal spatula. Immediately roll each cookie around the handle of a wooden spoon, holding in place a few seconds until cookie holds a cigarettelike shape. Set cookies aside to finish cooling. (Work quickly or the cookies will become too brittle to shape. Should this happen, place them in the oven for a few seconds to resoften.)

Continue to bake the rest of the batter in the same manner until all the cookies have been shaped.

Yield: 24 cookies

Note: These cookies are very sensitive to humidity. Therefore, they should be stored in an airtight container and used the day they are made.

1 cookie
Cholesterol: 0 mg Total Fat: 2 gm
Saturated Fat: 0 gm Calories: 29

A Celebration of Spring

Serves 6

Roasted Peppered Salmon
Lemon-Thyme Vinaigrette
Poached Asparagus
Blissful New Potatoes
Angel Food Cake Beaded with Berries

Roasted Peppered Salmon

Executive chef and cooking teacher Bob Posch invented this snappy salmon dish. The breading and quick roasting are clever techniques that make it easy to keep the fish moist. And the light, leafy Lemon-Thyme Vinaigrette (see next recipe) provides a commendable contrast to the salmon's delicate flavor. Tiny new potatoes and young asparagus complete a trio that is the very essence of spring.

In keeping with the elegance and simplicity of this meal, should you want a starter, why not Scottish smoked salmon with capers and toast?

> Six 6-ounce center-cut salmon fillets, pin bones and skin removed
> Extra-virgin olive oil for preparing salmon and pan
> 1 cup dry bread crumbs
> 1 teaspoon salt
> 1 tablespoon coarsely ground black pepper

Preheat oven to 400 degrees.

Lightly brush the entire surface of each piece of salmon with olive oil. In a bowl large enough to comfortably hold each fillet, combine the bread crumbs, salt, and pepper. Evenly coat each piece of fish with the mixture. Shake off any excess.

Grease a baking sheet lightly with olive oil. Arrange pieces of fish so they are not touching. Bake in preheated oven until done, 10–12 minutes, depending on the thickness of the fillets. (The cooked salmon should be moist and blush at its center.)

Transfer each fillet to a warmed dinner plate. Spoon a ribbon of Lemon-Thyme Vinaigrette over each portion. Pass additional vinaigrette in a sauceboat.

1 fillet, without sauce
Cholesterol: 95 mg   Total Fat: 12 gm
Saturated Fat: 2 gm   Calories: 292

Lemon-Thyme Vinaigrette

1/4 cup white vinegar
1/4 cup freshly squeezed lemon juice, strained
4 teaspoons Dijon mustard
1/2 teaspoon salt
2 tablespoons chopped fresh parsley
2 tablespoons chopped scallion
2 teaspoons fresh thyme leaves
1/2 cup extra-virgin olive oil

In the workbowl of a food processor, combine vinegar, lemon juice, mustard, salt, half the parsley, half the scallion, and half the thyme leaves. With the blade in motion, add the olive oil in a thin, continuous stream and process until smooth.

Pour the dressing into a small bowl and stir in the balance of the parsley, scallion, and thyme by hand.

Yield: 1 1/3 cups

1 tablespoon
Cholesterol: 0 mg   Total Fat: 5 gm
Saturated Fat: 1 gm   Calories: 45

Poached Asparagus

2 pounds medium asparagus
1 teaspoon salt

Snap or cut off the stems of the asparagus at the point where they become white in color and woody in texture. Using a vegetable peeler, peel the stalks from their midpoint to their cut end.

Using a wide shallow pan large enough to hold all the asparagus, bring 2 inches of water to a rapid boil. Add the salt. Carefully add the asparagus. Cook at a moderate boil for about 5 minutes. (Asparagus should be bright green and slightly crisp to the bite.)

Lift the asparagus from the water and place on a clean cloth to dry.

Serve warm.

Cholesterol: 0 mg   Total Fat: 0 gm
Saturated Fat: 0 gm   Calories: 26

Blissful New Potatoes

2 pounds small red bliss potatoes, of uniform size, well scrubbed
2 medium scallions, cleaned and finely minced
½ cup Lemon-Thyme Vinaigrette (see page 145)

In a large pot, cover potatoes with cold water. Over high heat, bring to a full boil. Immediately reduce heat. Simmer, partially covered, until tender, about 15 minutes.

Drain potatoes. Quarter them. (If potatoes are more than 2 inches long, cut them into more than 4 pieces.)

Combine potatoes, scallions, and vinaigrette.

Serve warm.

Cholesterol: 0 mg   Total Fat: 7 gm
Saturated Fat: 1 gm   Calories: 216

Angel Food Cake
Beaded with Berries

Several years ago, we were part of a food story in a popular New York weekly. A television news commentator, who spent much of her free time at spas keeping trim and fit, saw it and booked us for a ladies' lunch she was hosting. The menu had to be beautiful, delicious, healthy, and light. The day arrived and the meal began. The ladies were full of compliments but ate sparingly, as these ladies in TV and the press do. Then this dessert arrived. Not a crumb remained.

1 cup sifted cake flour
1½ cups granulated sugar
1¼ cups egg whites (about 10 eggs), at room temperature
1¼ teaspoons cream of tartar
¼ teaspoon salt
1 teaspoon pure vanilla extract
¼ teaspoon almond extract
2 cups fresh raspberries, washed
1¼ cups Raspberry Sauce (see page 241)

Preheat oven to 325 degrees.

Sift the flour with ½ cup of the sugar three times.

Beat the egg whites in the large bowl of an electric mixer until foamy. Add the cream of tartar and salt and beat until soft peaks form. Beat in the remaining 1 cup of sugar at high speed, about 2 tablespoons at a time, beating well after each addition. Beat in the vanilla and almond extracts. The egg whites will be stiff and glossy.

Sift about 4 tablespoons of the flour-sugar mixture at a time over the egg whites, and fold in by hand until no flour shows. Repeat until all of the flour-sugar mixture has been incorporated.

Pour batter into an ungreased angel food cake pan. Bake in the preheated oven until a toothpick inserted in the center comes out clean, about 1 hour. Remove from oven.

Invert the pan and let the cake cool completely before unmolding.

To serve, slice the cake in 8 pieces. Place a piece of angel food cake in the center of each of 6 dessert plates. Distribute berries evenly over each serving. Drizzle each portion with Raspberry Sauce. Pass remaining Raspberry Sauce separately.

1 slice cake with berries and 1 tablespoon sauce
Cholesterol: 0 mg   Total Fat: 0 gm
Saturated Fat: 0 gm   Calories: 240

A Seafood Supper

Serves 6

Pinzimonio
Snappy Breadsticks
Seafood Risotto
Herb Garden Salad
Cantaloupe Sorbet Slices

Pinzimonio

Pinzimonio refers to a popular Italian starter composed of a bouquet of raw vegetables served with a dipping sauce of first-quality olive oil. So if you have a special bottle of extra-virgin, now's the time to use it. This dish is perfect for dieters; those who must can nibble on the naked vegetables, while the luckier ones can sample the sauce. But take heed, just a little goes a long way.

1 cup extra-virgin olive oil
Coarse salt
Freshly ground black pepper
2 large fennel bulbs, trimmed and cut lengthwise into 8 wedges
1 medium bunch celery, separated into ribs with leaves attached
2 large sweet red peppers, cored, seeded, and cut lengthwise into 8
    segments
2 large sweet yellow peppers, cored, seeded, and cut lengthwise into 8
    segments
12 tiny artichokes, blanched

In a small serving bowl, thoroughly combine the olive oil with salt and pepper to taste.

Fill the bottom of a large serving bowl with crushed ice. Arrange the vegetables in it to resemble a bouquet. Serve with the bowl of dipping oil.

About 1 1/2 cups assorted vegetables, with 1 tablespoon sauce
Cholesterol: 0 mg   Total Fat: 13 gm
Saturated Fat: 2 gm   Calories: 174

Snappy Breadsticks

These skinny sticks are perfect with the Pinzimonio. Use them to surround the Pinzimonio bouquet for munching along with the vegetables. We do them in two flavors to add to the fun, which begins in the kitchen in the making.

1 package active dry yeast
7 tablespoons lukewarm water (between 100 and 115 degrees)
$\frac{1}{2}$ teaspoon granulated sugar
4 teaspoons anchovy paste
2 teaspoons extra-virgin olive oil, plus a few extra drops to oil bowl
$\frac{1}{4}$ teaspoon salt
2 tablespoons yellow cornmeal
1 cup all-purpose flour
Coarsely ground black pepper

Combine yeast, water, and sugar in a medium bowl. Stir to dissolve yeast. Let sit until mixture becomes foamy on surface, about 10 minutes.

Add the anchovy paste, 2 teaspoons olive oil, and salt. Stir with a whisk until the anchovy paste dissolves. Add cornmeal and flour. Mix with hands to form a smooth, slightly sticky ball of dough.

Place dough in a medium-size bowl with a few drops of oil. Turn the dough in the bowl to coat all sides with oil. Cover bowl with plastic wrap and set aside in a warm, draft-free place. Allow dough to double in bulk. This will take approximately 30 minutes.

Meanwhile, preheat oven to 350 degrees.

Line a sheet pan with aluminum foil and set aside.

When the dough has doubled in bulk, punch it down. Turn it out of the bowl onto a clean, dry work surface. Divide the dough into approximately eighteen $\frac{1}{2}$-ounce pieces. Roll each piece between the work surface and the palms of your hands to form a long, thin, snakelike shape. (It should be about 12 inches long and between $\frac{1}{8}$ inch and $\frac{1}{4}$ inch thick.)

Place half the breadsticks on the sheet pan, $\frac{1}{2}$ inch apart. Lightly sprinkle the remaining breadsticks with coarsely ground black pepper and roll the dough in it, until the pepper adheres. Place these breadsticks in the sheet pan as well.

Bake the breadsticks in the center of the preheated oven until lightly browned, about 15 minutes. Remove from oven and cool on a rack.

Yield: About 18 breadsticks

Note: Breadsticks may be stored in an airtight container for several days. The longer they are stored, the stronger the anchovy flavor becomes.

1 breadstick
Cholesterol: 0 mg   Total Fat: 1 gm
Saturated Fat: 0 gm   Calories: 36

Seafood Risotto

This attractive and elegant risotto is wonderful for a special occasion. It lends itself to low-cholesterol entertaining since it is made with olive oil instead of the usual butter, and it is one of the few risottos that require absolutely no cheese. Made with Lobster Stock and dotted with scallops, shrimp, and lobster meat, it is an overwhelming hit whenever we serve it. In fact, one of our regular clients, a well-known hostess with impeccable taste, serves it at every party.

4 tablespoons extra-virgin olive oil
1 large carrot, peeled and very finely diced
1 large celery rib, very finely diced
3 small shallots, peeled and finely chopped
2 cups Arborio rice
1 cup dry white wine
6 cups Lobster Stock (see page 237), brought to a boil
12 small shrimp, peeled and deveined
12 sea scallops, each cut into 2 medallions
Three 1½-pound lobsters, cooked, claw meat removed and reserved
    whole, tail meat removed and sliced into ¼-inch medallions
Salt
Freshly ground black pepper
1 tablespoon finely chopped fresh parsley

Heat 1 tablespoon of the oil in a large nonstick frying pan (10–12 inches in diameter) over medium heat. Add carrot and celery and sauté until tender, about 10 minutes. Set aside.

Heat 2 tablespoons of oil in a large saucepan (about 6-quart capacity) over medium heat. Sauté shallots until soft, about 5 minutes. Add the rice, stir to coat with oil, and heat through, about 1 minute. Add the wine and continue to stir occasionally, until the rice absorbs the liquid, about 5 minutes. Stirring constantly now, add the hot Lobster Stock, 1 cup at a time, waiting until each cup of liquid is absorbed before adding the next. (It should take a total of 20–25 minutes to incorporate all the stock.)

Fifteen minutes after adding the wine to the rice, stir in the cooked carrots and celery.

Pour the remaining 1 tablespoon of oil into the frying pan in which the carrots and celery were sautéed and heat over medium flame. Add the shrimp and scallops. Cook just until they turn opaque on each side, 4–5 minutes. Add lobster claw and tail meat. Continue to cook until heated through, about 3 minutes.

At this time the rice should also be cooked. It will be slightly chewy and have a consistency resembling oatmeal. Add salt and pepper to taste. Stir until well combined.

To serve, divide the rice evenly among 6 warm, shallow soup plates. Shape each portion into a mound. Place the meat of one lobster claw on top of each pile of rice. Divide the remaining seafood evenly and arrange it around the outer edge of each portion. Garnish with chopped parsley. Serve immediately.

Cholesterol: 167 mg   Total Fat: 12 gm
Saturated Fat: 2 gm   Calories: 532

Herb Garden Salad

Herbs in salads aren't anything new. But herbs *as* salads are. À la mode in France, these amalgams of fresh flavors are a tasty surprise as a substitute for the usual greens. Serve this salad as a separate course. Your guests will be intrigued and delighted.

2 teaspoons white wine vinegar
2 teaspoons balsamic vinegar
1 teaspoon whole-grain mustard
1 teaspoon grated lemon rind
2 tablespoons extra-virgin olive oil
Salt
Freshly ground black pepper
½ cup chervil leaf clusters, washed and dried
1 cup curly parsley leaf clusters, washed and dried

½ cup flatleaf parsley leaf clusters, washed and dried
½ cup mint leaves, washed and dried
½ cup chives, cut into 2-inch lengths, washed and dried

In a small bowl, combine the white wine and balsamic vinegars, mustard, and lemon rind. Stir with a whisk until well blended. Add the olive oil in a slow, thin stream, whisking continuously. When the oil is incorporated, season with salt and pepper. Reserve in the refrigerator.

Store herbs, loosely packed and tightly covered, in the refrigerator for at least 1 hour.

In a large bowl, toss the herbs to mix them and so that they are not densely packed. Toss again with 2 tablespoons of the vinaigrette.

To serve, mound a loosely packed half-cup of dressed herbs on the center of each of 6 chilled salad plates.

| Cholesterol: 0 mg | Total Fat: 4 gm |
| Saturated Fat: 1 gm | Calories: 49 |

Cantaloupe Sorbet Slices

It's hard to tell what guests like better about this dessert — its cool, refreshing taste or its whimsical presentation. A cantaloupe sorbet served in wedges of the original shell, it looks like a slice of the fruit itself, complete with seeds. Getting this to look right takes a bit of doing, so leave yourself enough time to experiment.

1 ripe, sweet cantaloupe
1 tablespoon freshly squeezed lemon juice
1 cup sugar syrup (made by dissolving ½ cup granulated sugar in ½ cup boiling water)
1 ounce semisweet chocolate

With a sharp knife, cut the cantaloupe into 8 equal segments. Remove all seeds and discard. Scoop out cantaloupe flesh, making sure not to include any green portion.

Reform each of the 8 shell segments, storing in a round-sided bowl to preserve the natural shape. Reserve in the freezer.

Meanwhile, puree the cantaloupe flesh in the workbowl of a food processor along with the lemon juice. Taste and add sugar syrup as necessary, to obtain desired sweetness.

Process the puree in an ice cream maker for 30–40 minutes, or according to manufacturer's advice.

Take a single frozen shell from the freezer. Lay it on its side on a piece of wax paper and fill it with the sorbet. Smooth the exposed side with a knife or spatula so that it resembles a cantaloupe slice. Leave it on its side on the wax paper and refreeze. Fill each of the shells in this manner. Freeze for several hours.

To decorate, melt the chocolate in a small saucepan and, using a pastry bag and plain tip, decorate each slice with several "seeds."

Yield: 8 slices

1 slice
Cholesterol: 0 mg   Total Fat: 1 gm
Saturated Fat: 1 gm   Calories: 90

Fine and Fancy

Serves 6

Tomato Consommé
Grilled Salmon
Pappardelle with Leeks
Leek and Lobster Sauce
Sautéed Baby Carrots
Radicchio and Endive Salad
Floating Islands

Tomato Consommé

A captain at New York's famous Lutèce restaurant was trying valiantly to sell one of the evening's specials as a first course, but my husband stood firm. He wanted the consommé. Finally the frustrated fellow relaxed and smiled. "You must be a chef," he said. He was right. Chefs know a consommé is the true test of a kitchen's worth. Its purity of flavor is unbeatable. Our clients need to be convinced to try this liquid gold, but after their first encounter, they become converts for life. This soup requires some work, but it is well worth it.

Two 28-ounce cans imported crushed plum tomatoes
1 large carrot, finely chopped
2 large shallots, peeled and finely chopped
1 small celery rib, finely chopped
1 large garlic clove, peeled and smashed
6 cups Beef Stock (see page 234)
1 teaspoon granulated sugar
¼ cup tomato paste
3 large egg whites
3 ice cubes
3 tablespoons gin
Salt
Freshly ground black pepper
1 large sweet red pepper, skin removed with a vegetable peeler, cored,
      seeded, and cut into small diamonds
1 large sweet yellow pepper, prepared in the same manner as red pepper
1 large tomato, peeled, seeded, and cut into small diamonds

In a medium stockpot (about 6-quart capacity) combine crushed tomatoes with their liquid, carrot, shallots, celery, garlic, Beef Stock, and sugar. Bring to a boil over high heat. Lower heat and simmer 40 minutes.

Remove from heat and cool to room temperature. Put soup in a container, cover tightly, and refrigerate several hours or overnight.

Return soup to medium stockpot.

In a small bowl, stir tomato paste, egg whites, and ice cubes with a whisk to combine. Add to the soup and place over medium heat. Stirring constantly, bring soup to a boil. Stop stirring. Reduce heat and allow to simmer 15 minutes.

Line a sieve with a kitchen towel. Pass soup through sieve. Discard solids that remain in towel.

Add the gin to the soup. Season with salt and pepper to taste.

To serve, heat soup thoroughly and pour into 6 warmed bowls. Garnish each bowl with diamonds of tomato and red and yellow pepper.

Cholesterol: 0 mg Total Fat: 1 gm
Saturated Fat: 0 gm Calories: 126

Grilled Salmon

Salmon, with its beautiful color, firm texture, and rich taste, is always the right choice. In this recipe, we grill it for the smoky flavor that complements the pappardelle and the Leek and Lobster Sauce we serve it with (see following recipes). But fish cooked in this simple, straightforward way is perfect all by itself. Invest in a high-quality ridged, nonstick grill pan. You can successfully grill poultry, fish, and vegetables, using little or no fat. And in no time you'll get the hang of those cross-hatching marks, which will leave you feeling just like a professional.

Since coordinating all the parts of the entrée for this menu takes a bit of doing, we've offered some pointers to help you organize your activities. Most especially, we want to remind you to read through all the recipes to be sure you understand them before beginning your preparations. Your reward will be in the result — a savory grilled salmon fillet resting on a bed of leek-and-lobster-sauced pasta and accented by a brilliant orange fan of baby carrots — a feast for the eyes as well as the palate.

Six 7-ounce salmon fillets, skin and bones removed
Salt
Freshly ground black pepper
Extra-virgin olive oil
Freshly squeezed juice of 1 lemon, strained

Preheat oven to 375 degrees.

Rub each fillet with salt, pepper, and a few drops of olive oil. Set aside.

Heat a grill pan over high flame until it just begins to smoke. Place salmon, a few fillets at a time, in pan and, lowering heat to medium, cook 2–3 minutes on each side to sear the fish. Remove to a foil-lined shallow baking dish.

In order to coordinate cooking time of salmon and pappardelle, wait until pasta has boiled about 3 minutes before continuing.

Place baking dish in preheated oven and cook 5–8 minutes. (Five minutes will produce a rare result, 8 minutes a well-done one.) Remove from oven and sprinkle fillets with lemon juice. Salmon is now ready to be placed on the pappardelle.

Cholesterol: 111 mg   Total Fat: 15 gm
Saturated Fat: 2 gm   Calories: 303

Pappardelle with Leeks

As a noodle nut, I take great pride in sleuthing out the perfect form of pasta for each recipe. I am convinced that making the right choice here adds significantly to the enjoyment of the dish. Here, the wide, meaty pappardelle add substance to the lightness of the fish while offering an ample foundation for the exquisite sauce. The filaments of leek that are threaded through the noodles offer color, texture, and just the right spark.

1 tablespoon salt, plus salt for seasoning leeks
2 tablespoons extra-virgin olive oil
3 medium leeks, white part only, cut in thin strips, washed thoroughly, drained, and dried
Freshly ground black pepper
One 8-ounce package imported pappardelle or tagliatelle noodles
3 cups Leek and Lobster Sauce (see next recipe)
6 fillets Grilled Salmon (see preceding recipe)
1 tablespoon finely chopped parsley

To cook pasta, in a large pot bring to a boil 3 quarts water to which 1 tablespoon salt has been added.

Meanwhile, heat 1 tablespoon olive oil in a large, nonstick frying pan over medium heat. Add the julienned leeks and salt and pepper to taste. Sauté until tender, stirring occasionally, about 10 minutes.

While the leeks are cooking, boil the pasta until al dente, about 7 minutes. (*To coordinate the parts of the entrée, start sautéeing the baby carrots (page 162) right after adding the pappardelle to boiling water. Put the salmon fillets in oven 3 minutes after the noodles have begun to cook.*)

When the pasta is done, drain it well, sprinkle with the remaining tablespoon of olive oil, and toss to coat evenly. Briefly set aside.

Add 1 cup Leek and Lobster Sauce to the sautéed leeks in the frying pan. Raise heat until the sauce comes to a boil. Immediately reduce heat and hold at a simmer until salmon is ready to serve. At the same time, in a saucepan bring the remaining 2 cups of sauce to a simmer.

Working quickly, add the pappardelle to the sauce-and-leek mixture in the frying pan. Toss to blend.

To serve, divide the pappardelle evenly among 6 warmed plates. Top each bed of noodles with a salmon fillet and approximately 1/3 cup hot Leek and Lobster Sauce. Garnish each serving with a bit of chopped parsley.

1 serving pappardelle before topping
with salmon and additional sauce
Cholesterol: 3 mg   Total Fat: 9 gm
Saturated Fat: 1 gm   Calories: 234

Leek and Lobster Sauce

I was introduced to this sauce at the home of Greg Case. Since I was not the only guest, and it was a special occasion, I ate the dish and assumed I would be forgiven this one night's cholesterol indiscretion. I don't know if I was more relieved or embarrassed (considering myself an expert on these matters) at learning that this sauce, a dead ringer for French haute cuisine, was made without a drop of butter or cream. It doesn't get any better than this. Serve the sauce with other kinds of fish, or on its own with your favorite pasta. Make sure to provide spoons, so guests can enjoy every last drop.

1 tablespoon extra-virgin olive oil
3 large leeks, white part only (about 10 ounces), split, washed, drained, and coarsely chopped
$^1/_2$ teaspoon freshly ground white pepper
2 teaspoons Pernod
2 cups Lobster Stock (see page 237)
$^1/_3$ cup Yogurt Cheese (see page 239)
Salt

In a medium saucepan, heat oil over medium heat, 1–2 minutes. Add leeks and pepper, stirring over heat, 2–3 minutes. Add Pernod. Stir briefly, then cover pot and cook over medium heat until leeks are very soft, about 5 minutes, stirring occasionally.

Add Lobster Stock. Bring to a boil. Reduce heat and simmer for 5 minutes, uncovered. Remove pan from heat. Stir in Yogurt Cheese.

Preferably using a blender (a food processor may also be used), liquefy the mixture in small batches, until very smooth. Return to the pan. Add salt to taste and keep sauce at low simmer until ready to serve.

Yield: 3 cups

$^1/_3$ cup
Cholesterol: 3 mg   Total Fat: 5 gm
Saturated Fat: 1 gm   Calories: 49

Sautéed Baby Carrots

We were never heavily into the baby vegetable craze — too precious! But these little carrots are an exception. Best in bunches, when they are at their freshest, they are also widely available in produce stores and supermarkets, trimmed and sealed in plastic bags. Good team players, they provide a harmonizing accompaniment rather than an individual statement, which makes them a perfect vegetable for this dramatic entrée.

1 teaspoon salt, plus salt for seasoning carrots

1¼ pounds baby carrots, peeled

3 tablespoons extra-virgin olive oil

2 teaspoons granulated sugar

2 teaspoons Dijon mustard

¼ cup finely chopped fresh parsley

Freshly ground black pepper

In a large pot, combine 1 quart water and 1 teaspoon salt. Add carrots and bring to a boil. Cook until barely tender, 5–7 minutes.

Using a colander, drain carrots and run under cold water to stop cooking. Set aside. (This step can be completed up to 1 hour in advance.)

To coordinate this dish with the other elements of the entrée, start the following portion of this recipe just after adding the pappardelle to the water to cook.

Heat olive oil in a large, nonstick frying pan. Add carrots, sugar, and mustard. Stir to coat carrots well. Add parsley. Add salt and pepper to taste.

Sauté until carrots are heated through, approximately 5 minutes. Taste for salt and pepper.

To serve, fan carrots pointing in the same direction, side by side, adjacent to the pappardelle and salmon.

Cholesterol: 0 mg   Total Fat: 7 gm
Saturated Fat: 1 gm   Calories: 106

Radicchio and Endive Salad

The combination of the ruby red radicchio and the ivory white endive make for a sophisticated salad that is chic enough to follow this entrée. Its texture and taste are enhanced by our favorite creamy vinaigrette, as good as it ever was when we used to make it with cream.

3 heads radicchio (about ¾ pound total)

3 heads endive (about ½ pound total)

Garlic Dressing (see below)
Salt
Freshly ground black pepper

Wash and dry lettuces. Gently tear into bite-size pieces. Place in a salad bowl.

Pour half the dressing over the salad. Toss. Add more dressing if necessary. Make sure the lettuces are well coated. Add salt and pepper to taste.

Note: The salad should be dressed just before serving. The radicchio and endive may be prepared but left undressed, and held in the refrigerator, covered with a damp paper towel, for several hours.

Serving includes about 1½ tablespoons dressing
Cholesterol: 0 mg   Total Fat: 15 gm
Saturated Fat: 2 gm   Calories: 158

GARLIC DRESSING

1 tablespoon egg white
2 teaspoons Dijon mustard
1 tablespoon freshly squeezed lemon juice, strained
2 tablespoons white wine vinegar (or plain vinegar)
1 small garlic clove, peeled and finely minced (about ¾ teaspoon)
Salt
Freshly ground black pepper
¼ cup canola (or other vegetable) oil
½ cup extra-virgin olive oil

In a medium-size bowl, whisk together all ingredients except the two oils.

In a slow, steady stream, pour vegetable oil into other ingredients, whisking constantly. Add the olive oil in the same manner. When the oils are incorporated, they will produce a creamy dressing. Taste for salt and pepper.

Cover the bowl with plastic wrap and refrigerate until ready to use.

Yield: About 1 cup

Note: The dressing will keep 2–3 days in the refrigerator. The garlic flavor will become more pronounced the longer the dressing stands.

1 tablespoon
Cholesterol: 0 mg   Total Fat: 10 gm
Saturated Fat: 2 gm   Calories: 97

Floating Islands

Floating islands are a classical French dessert that enjoyed wide popularity in the 1950s. These gossamer white meringues, sailing on a scarlet sea, provide a light but satisfying conclusion to an elegant meal like this. We like the stunning color and seasonal taste of raspberries for our sauce, but other colorful fruit sauces make excellent alternatives.

Although working with the mixture takes some getting used to, it is quite forgiving. Your mistakes can be remade, and the final product will impress your most discerning guest.

One 12-ounce can evaporated skim milk
1 vanilla bean, split lengthwise
5 large egg whites, at room temperature
²/₃ cup granulated sugar
1 cup Raspberry Sauce (see page 241)
Fresh mint leaves for garnish

In an 8–9-inch skillet, heat milk over low flame. Add the vanilla bean and continue to cook until bubbles begin to form around edge of pan.

Meanwhile, beat egg whites until soft peaks begin to form. Gradually add sugar while continuing to beat, until egg whites become a stiff meringue, 2–3 minutes more.

Using two large tablespoons that have been moistened with cold water, shape the meringue into egg-shaped mounds. Gently drop these, a few at a time, into the warm milk. Poach for 2 minutes. Using two rubber spatulas, gently flip the meringues and continue to poach for 2 minutes on the other side. (Be sure that the milk does not boil or the egg shape will be destroyed.) The meringues should be firm to the touch. Remove to a towel-lined tray to cool.

Repeat this method until all egg whites have been shaped and poached. (There will be a few extra meringues to allow for breakage.) Refrigerate the meringues, uncovered, until ready to serve.

To serve, place 2 tablespoons of Raspberry Sauce in a pool on each of 6 dessert plates. Float 2 meringues on top of sauce, on each plate. Drizzle a few parallel lines of raspberry sauce on top of each meringue. Garnish with mint leaves.

 Note: Poached meringues will keep several hours in the refrigerator.

Cholesterol: 0 mg Total Fat: 0 gm
Saturated Fat: 0 gm Calories: 185

SUMMER

A Beat-the-Heat Brunch

Serves 6

Cool Minestrone Soup
Niçoise Tart
Grapefruit Ice "Cream"

Cool Minestrone Soup

Years ago I was a guest at an outdoor feast at an Italian farmhouse in the Veneto. The host had quite a reputation as a cook, so I was dumbfounded when he served his soup cold. I admired the restraint and politeness of the assembled guests, who emptied their bowls as if nothing were wrong. I was embarrassed at learning later that nothing was. Cool minestrone is a popular summer soup in Italy.

This fine rendition is a creation of chef Richard Malanga, derived from one his mother used to serve on Fridays. It is simple to make, and since it gets better as it sits, can be made ahead. It's an endlessly versatile dish. The vegetables, pasta, and beans may be varied with felicitous results. Serve it hot or cool, as a starter (as we do here) or as a supper. Buòn appetito!

¹/₄ cup extra-virgin olive oil

2 medium carrots, peeled and cut into small dice

2 celery ribs, strings removed and cut into small dice

1 medium onion, peeled and cut into small dice

1 medium leek, white part only, washed thoroughly and cut into small dice

1 medium zucchini, cut into small dice

1 cup sliced white cabbage (Swiss chard or escarole may be substituted)

¹/₂ cup diced string beans and/or ¹/₂ cup frozen green peas

1 medium yellow squash, diced

2 large garlic cloves, peeled and diced

¹/₂ teaspoon dried thyme

¹/₂ teaspoon dried oregano

¹/₂ teaspoon dried sage

Pinch of sugar dissolved in ¹/₄ cup red wine

8 fresh basil leaves

2 tablespoons chopped Italian (flatleaf) parsley

2 medium tomatoes, peeled, seeds removed, and diced (canned may be substituted)

3–4 cups Chicken Stock (see page 235)

3–4 cups Beef Stock (see page 234)

10 ounces canned cannelini beans, drained

1 cup cooked tubettini macaroni
Extra-virgin olive oil
Parmesan cheese for grating

In a large noncorrosive soup pot heat the ¼ cup olive oil. Add the carrots, celery, onion, and leek. Cover, and cook for about 10 minutes on a low flame, being careful not to brown the vegetables. Add the zucchini, cabbage, string beans and/or peas, yellow squash, garlic, thyme, oregano, sage, sugar dissolved in wine, basil, and parsley and cook for another 5 minutes until these vegetables soften a bit.

Add the tomatoes, Chicken Stock, and Beef Stock and allow to simmer for 30–60 minutes.

Toward the end of the cooking time, add the cannelini beans and macaroni and allow them to heat through. Remove soup from heat and allow to cool.

Serve at room temperature accompanied by a bottle of extra-virgin olive oil and a wedge of Parmesan cheese for grating.

Cholesterol: 0 mg   Total Fat: 11 gm
Saturated Fat: 1 gm   Calories: 313

Niçoise Tart

I've heard of people with perfect food memories. They remember every meal they've ever eaten. I can't claim that kind of recall, but I do have a pretty long list of memorable dishes. About twenty years ago, at the height of the quiche era, I was at a brunch where the hostess served one she had found in Perla Meyers's *Seasonal Kitchen*. I never forgot it. In fact, I recently met Ms. Meyers and was pleased to finally have the opportunity to thank her. The memory of that wonderful tart provided the inspiration for this one, which is made without butter, whole milk, or egg yolks. Serve it hot or at room temperature.

For the Savory Pastry Dough:

2 cups all-purpose flour
1 teaspoon salt
⅓ cup canola (or other vegetable) oil

⅓ cup extra-virgin olive oil

1½ tablespoons dry white wine

1½ tablespoons evaporated skim milk

For the filling:

3 tablespoons extra-virgin olive oil

1 small eggplant, peeled, cubed, and salted, then drained for 1 hour

1 large onion, peeled and diced

1 large sweet yellow pepper, cored, seeded, and diced

1 large garlic clove, peeled and minced

One 14½-ounce can peeled whole Italian plum tomatoes, drained,
    crushed, and drained again

1 cup evaporated skim milk

1 bay leaf

1½ teaspoons anchovy paste

2 tablespoons all-purpose flour

2 tablespoons dry white vermouth

1 tablespoon finely chopped fresh basil

¼ cup niçoise olives, pitted and coarsely chopped

Salt

Freshly ground black pepper

To make the pastry dough, combine the flour and salt in a large bowl. Stir with a whisk until well combined. Make a well in the center of the dry ingredients. Add the canola and olive oils, white wine, and evaporated skim milk. Stir the liquid ingredients together with a whisk.

Using your fingers, quickly work the dry ingredients into the liquid until a ball forms.

Place the dough into a 10-inch tart pan or pie dish. Using fingertips, press the dough evenly over bottom and sides of pan. Place dough-lined dish in freezer for 15 minutes.

While the dough chills, preheat oven to 450 degrees.

When the tart shell has chilled, place it in the center of the preheated oven and bake until bottom and sides are golden brown, 15–20 minutes. Remove from oven and cool on a rack.

Reduce oven temperature to 350 degrees.

To make the filling, heat 2 tablespoons of the olive oil in a large nonstick skillet (10–12 inches in diameter) over high heat until it just begins to smoke.

Blot the eggplant dry with paper toweling, add it to the skillet, and reduce heat to medium high. Cook until well-browned on all sides, about 10 minutes. Using a slotted spoon, remove eggplant to a plate lined with several layers of paper towels. Set aside to drain.

Add remaining tablespoon olive oil to the same skillet. Over medium heat, add onion, yellow pepper, and garlic. Cook until pepper is soft and onion is translucent, about 10 minutes. Add the tomatoes and continue to cook until mixture achieves a dry, pastelike consistency, about 15 minutes more.

Meanwhile, in a medium saucepan (about 2-quart capacity) heat the evaporated skim milk, bay leaf, and anchovy paste over low heat.

While the mixture is heating, dissolve the flour in the vermouth. Using a whisk, stir the flour mixture into the warm milk. Stirring constantly, raise the heat to medium high and cook until the mixture boils and thickens, 3–4 minutes. Continue to stir and boil a minute longer. Remove from heat and cool slightly. Remove bay leaf and discard.

When the tomato mixture has reduced to a paste, stir it into the thickened milk. Add the eggplant, basil, and olives. Stir to combine. Add salt and pepper to taste.

Pour the filling into the prebaked tart shell and spread evenly over the bottom of the crust. Wrap a strip of aluminum foil around the outside of the tart pan and fold the edge so that it just covers the rim of the pastry crust. (This will prevent the pastry from browning too quickly.)

Bake the tart in the center of the 350-degree oven until the filling is set and lightly browned, about 1 hour. Remove from oven and cool on a rack 5 minutes before serving.

Cholesterol: 1 mg   Total Fat: 32 gm
Saturated Fat: 4 gm   Calories: 513

Grapefruit Ice "Cream"

I was a college girl in the days when bohemia was the height of sophistication. This exotic world was introduced to me in the person of Ann Rower, the ex-wife (even *that* was sophisticated) of a poet friend. From her sultry voice to her colorful costumes to the dishes on her table, her sense of style was unique. I still remember the first time I was a guest at her house — she served a lunch of chicken livers (first experience) sautéed in butter (old friend) with fresh mushrooms (first experience) and sour cream (old friend). I thought I had died and gone to heaven. Not being familiar with cholesterol and saturated fat at that time, I didn't know how close I had come.

This refreshing dessert is a current example of her talent and taste.

4 cups freshly squeezed grapefruit juice
8 ounces plain low-fat yogurt
2 large egg whites
½ cup plus 2 tablespoons granulated sugar

In a bowl large enough to hold all the ingredients, combine grapefruit juice, yogurt, egg whites, and sugar.

Pour into the container of an ice cream maker and mix according to manufacturer's instructions for 15–20 minutes.

Cholesterol: 5 mg	Total Fat: 1 gm
Saturated Fat: 0.7 gm	Calories: 167

A Provençal Lunch

Serves 6

Vin d'Orange

Grand Aioli

Olive Bread

Summer Fruit Pudding

. Biscotti Napoletani

Vin d'Orange

A Provençal aperitif is the perfect beginning to this meal. And what better one than Vin d'Orange, a summery wine cooler that is made from rosé steeped with orange rind. Make it well ahead. The flavor improves the longer the ingredients mingle. And serve it in a clear glass pitcher, since its beauty should be enjoyed. Offer it as we do, with little bowls of various kinds of olives, all the hors d'oeuvres you'll need.

Rind of 4 medium oranges, stripped with a vegetable peeler
One 750-milliliter bottle rosé wine
$1/2$ cup cognac
$1/2$ cup granulated sugar

Add strips of orange rind to the rosé wine in the bottle. Recork bottle and set aside in a cool place for 15 days.

Several hours before serving, mix the rosé wine and orange rind with the cognac and sugar in a large pitcher. Stir to mix, then refrigerate.

Serve chilled.

6 ounces
Cholesterol: 0 mg   Total Fat: 0 gm
Saturated Fat: 0 gm   Calories: 186

Grand Aioli

It was in Hyères, a beautiful town in the south of France, that I had my first encounter with a grand aioli, a glorious platter of Provençal summer food — cod, chicken, shrimp, and vegetables — as beautiful as it was delicious. But what stands out most in my memory is the taste of the sauce from which the dish gets its name. Could it be? Mayonnaise, a favorite since childhood, married to garlic, a best friend. We have been serving this dish ever since, and I can think of no greater crowd pleaser. We've altered the mayonnaise, so it is no longer a cholesterol concern. But we haven't touched the garlic.

1 salt cod fillet, 20 inches long

3 whole chicken legs, poached, skinned, and cut in half

12 prawns (with heads on) or large shrimp, poached

6 small red potatoes, boiled

6 small white potatoes, boiled

1/2 pound string beans, boiled

12 baby artichokes, trimmed and boiled until tender

1 small eggplant, cut into 1/4-inch slices, oiled, and grilled

1 sweet red pepper, cored, seeded, and sliced into wide strips

1 sweet yellow pepper, cored, seeded, and sliced into wide strips

1 fennel bulb, sliced into 1/4-inch rounds

18 fresh fava beans, in pods

12 small carrots, peeled

2 cups Aioli Sauce (see below)

To prepare salt cod, cut it into two equal pieces, put them in a bowl, and cover with cold water. Refrigerate for 24 hours, changing water frequently.

Put 2 quarts water in a deep 10-inch skillet. Drain cod and rinse it in cold water. Add to skillet and simmer for 10 minutes.

Gently remove cod from skillet and drain on several thicknesses of paper towels. Allow to cool before serving.

To serve, attractively arrange poultry, vegetables, and fish on one or several platters or bowls. Serve the Aioli Sauce in a bowl and let guests help themselves.

Not including Aioli Sauce
Cholesterol: 70 mg   Total Fat: 2 gm
Saturated Fat: 1 gm   Calories: 354

AIOLI SAUCE

1 large garlic clove, peeled and smashed

2 extra-large egg whites, at room temperature, beaten until foamy

4 teaspoons Dijon mustard

2 tablespoons rice wine vinegar (or plain vinegar)

1/2 teaspoon salt

1/8 teaspoon freshly ground white pepper

1 cup extra-virgin olive oil

6 tablespoons canola (or other vegetable) oil

3 tablespoons freshly squeezed lemon juice, strained

In the workbowl of a food processor combine garlic, egg whites, mustard, vinegar, salt, and pepper. Pulse several times to combine. With machine running, add the oils in a thin, slow, steady stream. When all the oil is incorporated it will create a thick sauce of mayonnaiselike consistency. Add the lemon juice, and adjust salt and pepper.

Using a rubber spatula, remove aioli to a bowl. Refrigerate at least 1 hour before serving.

Yield: About 2 cups

Note: Aioli Sauce will keep several days in refrigerator, tightly covered. The longer it sits, the stronger its garlic flavor.

1 tablespoon
Cholesterol: 0 mg   Total Fat: 10 gm
Saturated Fat: 1 gm   Calories: 90

Olive Bread

This spunky bread is just right with this food. Making it into a loaf that needs to be shared adds to the spirit of the party. It makes a great pizza dough as well, baked with fresh tomatoes and rosemary. And if you can find some low-fat goat cheese to add to the pizza, all the better.

1 package active dry yeast
1 cup warm water (100–115 degrees)
1 tablespoon extra-virgin olive oil, plus oil to grease bowl and sheet pan
1/2 cup niçoise olives, pitted and coarsely chopped
2 cups all-purpose flour, plus an additional 1/2 cup for kneading

Dissolve yeast in warm water in a medium-size mixing bowl.

Add 1 tablespoon olive oil, olives, and 2 cups flour. Mix with hands until well combined.

Turn dough out onto a floured board. Using remaining 1/2 cup flour to keep dough from sticking to board, knead until dough is smooth and elastic, about 10 minutes. The dough should remain soft and slightly sticky.

Place dough in an oiled bowl and turn to coat with oil. Cover bowl tightly with plastic wrap. Set aside in a warm, draft-free place. Allow to double in bulk, about 1 1/2 hours.

When the dough is twice its original size, punch it down. Remove it from bowl and divide into 12 equal portions. Shape each one into a smooth ball.

Arrange the dough balls in a circle on an oiled baking sheet, placing them about 1/2 inch apart. Cover with a damp towel. Set aside in a warm place to again double, about 40 minutes.

Preheat oven to 375 degrees.

When dough has doubled in bulk, bake it in the center of the preheated oven until it is well browned and sounds hollow when tapped, about 45 minutes.

Remove bread from oven. Wrap immediately in a damp towel. Allow to cool in towel until crust has softened and bread has reached room temperature.

To serve, remove bread from towel and place on a serving tray. Allow guests to break off individual rounds of bread.

Note: Bread is best eaten the day it is baked.

1 round
Cholesterol: 0 mg   Total Fat: 2 gm
Saturated Fat: 0 gm   Calories: 91

Summer Fruit Pudding

Greg, our dessert chef, had long resisted the idea of a soaked-bread base for a fruit dessert. So it was with great reluctance that he began to develop this recipe. But he rose to the challenge and was as surprised as anyone with the delectable result. Plum-puddinglike in texture, although wetter and juicier, blue-violet in hue, this dessert is hard to identify when you're eating it. But it's so good you don't care.

1 loaf Portuguese-Style Sweet Bread (see page 138) baked in a
     .10 x 4 1/2 x 3-inch loaf pan, sliced about 1/4 inch thick, crusts removed
1/2 cup granulated sugar
Zest of 1 lime, finely grated

¼ cup fresh lime juice, strained

½ cup water

2 cups blueberries, stemmed and drained

1 cup Bing cherries, pitted and coarsely chopped

1 cup strawberries, hulled and quartered

1 cup raspberries

Line a round-bottomed bowl (capacity 4–5 cups) with plastic wrap. Leave enough extra wrap hanging over one edge to later cover the top. Line the bowl with sliced bread. Trim small pieces and use them to fill in any gaps, making sure bowl is completely lined with bread. Save some bread to cover top. Set bread-lined bowl and extra bread aside.

Combine the sugar, lime zest and juice, water, blueberries, cherries, and strawberries in a medium saucepan (about 3-quart capacity). Place pan over high heat and bring contents to a boil. Reduce heat and simmer for 10 minutes. Stir occasionally.

Remove pan from heat. Strain off ¾ cup liquid and set aside. Pour remaining fruit and liquid into the bread-lined bowl. Cover the top with as much of the remaining bread as is needed, trimming and fitting to cover entire surface. (Leftover bread can be frozen, or used for another purpose.)

Fold plastic wrap over the top layer of bread. On top of the plastic wrap place a small plate that neatly fits within the rim of the bowl. Place a 1-pound weight on top of the saucer. Refrigerate pudding at least 6 hours, or preferably over-night, before serving.

While the pudding chills, make a sauce by pureeing the raspberries with the ¾ cup cooking liquid previously reserved. Pass puree through a fine sieve to remove seeds. Chill sauce until ready to serve.

To serve, remove weight and plate from bowl. Fold back plastic wrap. Invert bowl onto serving platter. Use plastic wrap to pull pudding out of bowl onto plate. Remove plastic wrap. Pour a little sauce over the top of the pudding, allowing it to run down the sides. Serve remaining sauce on the side.

Cholesterol: 1 mg   Total Fat: 4 gm
Saturated Fat: 0.5 gm   Calories: 331

Biscotti Napoletani

Biscotti are the cookies for the nineties — good-looking, not too sweet, and hard enough to chew that you feel you're getting your exercise. Dipped in a cup of espresso or a glass of Vin Santo, a syrupy Italian dessert wine, they are a perfect finale to a good meal.

We got the inspiration for our eggless version from one made by friend and master baker Nick Malgieri in his wonderful book *Great Italian Desserts*.

1 cup all-purpose flour
6 tablespoons granulated sugar
1/3 cup whole, unblanched almonds, finely ground
1/4 teaspoon baking powder
1/4 teaspoon baking soda
1/8 teaspoon ground cinnamon
1/3 cup whole, unblanched almonds
3 tablespoons light corn syrup
3 tablespoons water

Preheat oven to 350 degrees.

To a mixing bowl add flour, sugar, ground almonds, baking powder, baking soda, cinnamon, and whole almonds. Stir to combine. Add the corn syrup and water and mix to form a firm dough.

Remove dough from bowl. Roll into a 15-inch log. Place the log on a sheet pan lined with aluminum foil. Bake in the center of the preheated oven until golden brown, about 30 minutes.

Remove log from oven. Cool slightly. Place log on cutting board and slice diagonally at 1/2-inch intervals.

Return cut biscotti to sheet pan, cut side down, and bake until lightly browned, about 15 minutes more. Remove from oven and cool on the pan.

Yield: 24 biscotti

Note: Biscotti will keep several weeks in an airtight tin.

1 cookie
Cholesterol: 0 mg   Total Fat: 2 gm
Saturated Fat: 2 gm   Calories: 59

Burger Deluxe

Serves 6

Fresh Tuna Burgers
Unbeatable Buns
Tomato-Pepper Relish
Sweet Potato Fries
Coleslaw
Iced Tea
Lemonade
Brownies

Fresh Tuna Burgers

I was prepared to give up many things to preserve my health. But burgers? I had not had one in four years, but like a reformed alcoholic, I dreamed about them, encouraged friends to order them, and on more than one occasion, found myself seated at a luncheonette counter, dangerously close to the grill.

Well, burgers are back — classic taste with less cholesterol. But as with any magic, you must follow the directions exactly; the technique is essential to preserve the flavor. So break out the catsup, pickles, onions, and relish.

2 pounds fresh tuna, skinned and boned
Salt
Freshly ground black pepper
Canola (or other vegetable) oil

Using a large knife, coarsely chop tuna until the pieces are pea-size. (This may also be done in a food processor, but be careful not to grind too fine.) Sprinkle the fish with salt and pepper to taste. Shape into 6 burgers of equal size. Set aside. (If tuna burgers are not to be cooked immediately, refrigerate until ready to begin.)

In a large nonstick frying pan, heat a few drops of oil over medium-high heat until the oil just begins to smoke. Place 3 of the burgers in the pan, and cook until the first side is brown and crisp, 3–4 minutes. Flip burgers and continue to cook until browned on the other side, another 3–4 minutes. Remove cooked burgers to a warm tray and loosely cover with aluminum foil.

Add a few more drops of oil to the frying pan and cook remaining burgers in the same manner.

Note: These burgers are best when the center is rare, so make sure the fish is very fresh to begin with, then be sure oil is very hot and cooking time is brief.

Cholesterol: 68 mg   Total Fat: 6 gm
Saturated Fat: 0 gm   Calories: 203

Unbeatable Buns

The perfect burger deserves the perfect bun. Here it is, to rival any in your memory, just like the best of what you recall from the family picnic table. The hint of sweetness offsets the great "beefy" taste of what's inside.

1¼ cups warm skim milk (110–115 degrees)
1 package active dry yeast
2 tablespoons granulated sugar
3 tablespoons canola (or other vegetable) oil, plus oil to grease bowl and
    baking sheet
1 teaspoon salt
1 extra-large egg white
3–3½ cups all-purpose flour
Sesame seeds

In a large mixing bowl, combine milk, yeast, and sugar. Stir to dissolve yeast. Let stand until foamy, about 10 minutes.

Stir in oil, salt, and egg white, and mix thoroughly. Beat in the flour, 1 cup at a time, until a soft, slightly sticky dough forms.

Turn dough out of bowl onto a lightly floured surface and knead until very elastic, about 10 minutes.

Form dough into a ball and place in a lightly oiled bowl. Turn to coat evenly with oil and cover with plastic wrap. Set bowl aside in a warm, draft-free place and allow to rise until doubled in bulk, about 1 hour.

Punch down the dough thoroughly. Cover the bowl again and let the dough rise until double, about 30 minutes.

Punch down the dough, remove it from the bowl, and place it on a lightly floured surface. Divide into 6 equal portions and shape into balls. Press each ball flat into a round 4 inches in diameter.

Place buns on a lightly oiled baking sheet, 1 inch apart. Brush with water and sprinkle with sesame seeds. Lightly press down the seeds to help them adhere.

Cover with a towel and set aside to rise until doubled, about 20 minutes. While the buns rise, preheat the oven to 400 degrees. Remove towel from tray and bake buns on the center rack of oven until golden brown, about 20 minutes.

Remove from oven and cool on a rack.

Serve at room temperature.

Yield: 6 buns

Note: These buns may be frozen several months, so consider making a double recipe and freezing some for a later occasion.

Cholesterol: 1 mg   Total Fat: 8 gm
Saturated Fat: 1 gm   Calories: 334

Tomato-Pepper Relish

While all of the fixings for your burgers can come out of the supermarket, try this relish if you have the time. It's sweet and tangy, bright with summer color, and livelier than one found in a bottle. It makes a great low-fat salad dressing, or a zippy garnish for grilled fish. And put up in your own jars, it's a welcome present any time of year.

2 large tomatoes, peeled, seeded, and diced
1 large sweet yellow pepper, cored, seeded, and diced
1 large red onion, peeled and diced
1 large garlic clove, peeled and minced
1 teaspoon black mustard seeds
$1/4$ teaspoon ground turmeric
$1/4$ teaspoon ground cumin
1 teaspoon salt
$1/4$ cup granulated sugar
2 tablespoons tomato paste
1 small jalapeño pepper, seeded and finely chopped
$3/4$ cup malt vinegar

Combine tomatoes, yellow pepper, onion, garlic, mustard seeds, turmeric, cumin, salt, sugar, tomato paste, and jalapeño in a medium stockpot with a nonreactive lining, preferably stainless steel or enamel. Cover pot with lid and let stand at room temperature for 3 hours.

Uncover pot and place over medium-high heat. Stir in vinegar and bring to a boil. Reduce heat and simmer until mixture becomes thick, about 45 minutes.

Spoon hot relish into sterilized jars and allow to cool. Place lids on jars and refrigerate until ready to use.

Yield: 3 cups

Note: Relish is best when kept a week or more before serving. It can be kept in the refrigerator for several months.

> *2 tablespoons*
> Cholesterol: 0 mg   Total Fat: 0 gm
> Saturated Fat: 0 gm   Calories: 15

Sweet Potato Fries

The food world is in the middle of a fry craze. If it's a vegetable, cut it in sticks and deep-fry it. No wonder! Everybody loves fries, and they're cost effective. But they're also loaded with fat. The ones that we serve are different. While they retain the allure of the fry, we bake them in the oven using a fraction of the usual oil. We like ones made with sweet potatoes alongside our burgers. And our guests enjoy the unexpected in this otherwise classic meal.

6 small sweet potatoes, peeled and finely julienned (about 1/8 inch thick)
2 tablespoons all-purpose flour
1/4 cup extra-virgin olive oil
Salt

Preheat oven to 500 degrees.

Sprinkle potatoes with flour and toss to coat evenly. Set aside.

Pour oil onto a large, nonstick sheet pan (approximately 18 x 14 inches). Place potatoes on pan. Toss in the oil and sprinkle with salt. Place pan on top shelf of oven. Bake for 7 minutes.

Remove from oven and turn potatoes. Return to oven and continue to bake until potatoes have finished browning, about 7 minutes more.

Serve immediately.

> Cholesterol: 0 mg   Total Fat: 9 gm
> Saturated Fat: 1 gm   Calories: 195

Coleslaw

As with the rest of this menu, we wanted the coleslaw to taste authentic. The job wasn't easy, since the creamy kind we all remember was loaded with mayo. But using our low-cholesterol Mayonnaise, we got the flavor right without compromising our heart-healthy standards. Now if we only had some of those little pleated paper cups.

1 medium head green cabbage (about 1½ pounds), cored and shredded
¾ teaspoon salt
1½ teaspoons granulated sugar
1 teaspoon white wine vinegar (or plain vinegar)
3 large carrots, peeled and shredded
¾ cup Mayonnaise (see page 238)

Place cabbage in a colander and toss with the salt. Allow to drain for at least 1 hour.

Remove cabbage to a bowl and mix with sugar and vinegar. Add carrots and Mayonnaise. Toss to coat salad thoroughly with dressing.

Chill 1 hour before serving.

Note: Coleslaw will keep refrigerated, tightly covered, for several hours. Retoss before serving.

Cholesterol: 0 mg   Total Fat: 18 gm
Saturated Fat: 2 gm   Calories: 200

Iced Tea

We like to offer guests a choice of beverages with their burgers. We always have lots of beer on hand — regular, light, and alcohol-free — and, of course, our Lemonade (next recipe). But it wouldn't be summer without iced tea. This one is made with a blend of teas, combining herb and fruit flavors. Garnish tall, frosty glasses with a sprig of fresh mint for a perfect summertime thirst quencher.

2 quarts water
4 bags herbal lemon tea
6 bags orange pekoe tea
1 large navel orange, sliced into rounds

In a large stockpot, bring water to a boil. Remove pot from heat and add tea bags. Steep tea just until water becomes flavored, about 6 minutes. (The longer the tea sits in the hot water, the stronger the tannic acid flavor.)

Remove tea bags. Discard. Add orange slices and allow tea to cool to room temperature. Pour into a pitcher and refrigerate until chilled before serving.

Yield: 2 quarts

8 ounces
Cholesterol: 0 mg   Total Fat: 0 gm
Saturated Fat: 0 gm   Calories: 13

Lemonade

We want to share our favorite recipe for lemonade with you. We know of no other approach that avoids the problem of the sugar sinking to the bottom of the glass. The secret is to use a sugar syrup. We get the most mileage from our lemons by choosing ones that are soft and pliant. And we roll them hard on the counter surface before squeezing, to release the maximum juice. While we are always sure to include a pitcher of lemonade for any children in the party, the grown-ups are invariably our best customers.

10 cups water
1 cup granulated sugar
2 cups freshly squeezed lemon juice, strained (about 15 large lemons)
Coarsely chopped rind of 2 large lemons
1 large lemon, thinly sliced

In a small saucepan combine 2 cups water with 1 cup sugar. Slowly bring to a boil. Reduce heat and simmer 5 minutes.

Meanwhile, combine remaining 8 cups water, lemon juice, and lemon rind in a large pitcher.

Add the boiled sugar water and refrigerate several hours until well chilled. Before serving, use a slotted spoon to remove lemon rind.

To serve, fill tall glasses with ice and pour in lemonade. Garnish each glass with a lemon slice.

Yield: 3 quarts

8 ounces
Cholesterol: 0 mg   Total Fat: 0 gm
Saturated Fat: 0 gm   Calories: 73

Brownies

There are meals for which only one dessert makes sense. This is one. It has to be brownies. But a low-cholesterol brownie? We figured we'd just have to think of something else. We couldn't, so we decided to give it a try. A number of our initial efforts tasted just the way you might imagine. The dog wasn't even interested. But we persevered. When we finally got it right, I was so excited I couldn't sleep. (I was up all night eating the brownies.)

Solid vegetable shortening
2 cups all-purpose flour, plus flour to dust the pan
$\frac{1}{2}$ teaspoon salt
$\frac{1}{2}$ teaspoon baking soda
2 cups dark brown sugar
1 cup cocoa powder (Dutch processed)
$\frac{3}{4}$ cup coffee, hot and freshly brewed
$\frac{1}{2}$ cup canola (or other vegetable) oil
1 tablespoon pure vanilla extract
4 egg whites, lightly beaten
$\frac{1}{2}$ cup walnuts, coarsely chopped

Preheat oven to 350 degrees.

Grease an 8 x 10-inch baking pan with vegetable shortening and dust with flour. Invert pan and tap bottom to eliminate excess flour. Set aside.

Into a medium bowl sift 2 cups flour, salt, and baking soda. Set aside.

In a large bowl combine brown sugar, cocoa, coffee, oil, and vanilla extract. Stir until a smooth paste forms. (Mash any lumps of sugar or cocoa with the back of a spoon.) Stir in egg whites. Add dry ingredients to the chocolate mixture, stirring just enough to combine. Fold in nuts.

Pour batter into prepared pan. Bake in center of oven 25 minutes. (For a drier, cakier brownie continue baking until a toothpick inserted into the center comes out clean, about 5 minutes more.)

Yield: 20 brownies (2 x 2 inches)

1 brownie
Cholesterol: 0 mg   Total Fat: 9 gm
Saturated Fat: 2 gm   Calories: 233

A Spicy Sampler

Serves 6

Grilled Gazpacho Shrimp
Ancho Chicken Stew
Yellow Squash and Corn Scramble
Angel Biscuits
Grapefruit, Jicama, and Endive Salad
Bananas Baked in Phyllo with Caramel Sauce

Grilled Gazpacho Shrimp

Shrimp are back. Once considered high on the list of cholesterol crimi-nals, they are again on the table, thanks to their nutritional value and mi-nuscule saturated fat content. As a shrimp lover I am personally delighted; as a caterer, professionally grateful. Shrimp are the single most successful food at any party.

In this easy starter we grill the shrimp and serve them with a sauce inspired by gazpacho, the popular cold summer soup. If portions are doubled, this dish also makes a great lunch, sitting on a plate of crunchy greens.

18 large shrimp, peeled and deveined
5 tablespoons extra-virgin olive oil
Salt
Freshly ground black pepper
2 medium cucumbers, peeled, seeded, and very finely diced
2 small shallots, peeled and very finely chopped
1 medium garlic clove, peeled and minced
1 small sweet red pepper, cored, seeded, and very finely diced
4 teaspoons red wine vinegar
$\frac{1}{2}$ teaspoon cayenne pepper

In a medium bowl combine shrimp, 1 tablespoon oil, salt, and pepper to taste. Set aside.

In another medium bowl, make gazpacho sauce by combining cucumber, shallots, garlic, red pepper, vinegar, and cayenne pepper. Stir to combine. Add salt to taste. Set aside.

Heat a nonstick ridged grill pan over high heat until it just begins to smoke. Reduce heat to medium. Place shrimp on pan and grill 2 minutes. Turn each shrimp over and continue to cook until done, 3–4 minutes longer.

Meanwhile, portion the gazpacho sauce into mounds in the center of 6 salad plates. When the shrimps are cooked, place 3 on each mound of sauce. Serve immediately.

Cholesterol: 182 mg   Total Fat: 13 gm
Saturated Fat: 2 gm   Calories: 217

Ancho Chicken Stew

This lively Southwestern chicken dish gets its zing and rich terra-cotta color from cayenne pepper and ancho chili paste. Its engaging texture comes from hominy, a grain little known outside the South. Made from corn kernels that have been processed to remove the hull and germ, hominy in its canned form resembles tiny, bite-size dumplings. It gives stews like this one extra body. Don't look for it in your local gourmet shop, as I first did. You'll pay through the nose. Instead, check in the Spanish foods or canned foods section of your local supermarket. It's always been there and the price is right.

3 tablespoons extra-virgin olive oil
2 small chickens (2–3 pounds each), skin removed, cut into serving-size
    pieces
3 large garlic cloves, peeled and minced
1 large onion, peeled and finely chopped
2 cups Chicken Stock (see page 235)
One 28-ounce can imported crushed plum tomatoes
Two 12-ounce cans white hominy, drained
1/8 teaspoon cayenne pepper
4 large dried ancho chilies, soaked in water for 1 hour, drained, seeded,
    stemmed, and pureed with just enough soaking liquid to make a paste
3 tablespoons finely chopped fresh coriander (cilantro)
Salt
Freshly ground black pepper

Heat the olive oil in a large deep skillet (about 11 inches in diameter) over a high flame. Brown all the chicken, a few pieces at a time. Reserve browned chicken on a platter.

Without cleaning, use the same skillet and oil to cook the garlic and onions over medium heat until onions are soft, about 10 minutes.

Add the Chicken Stock, crushed tomatoes and their liquid, hominy, and cayenne pepper. Simmer over medium heat, stirring occasionally, for 20 minutes.

Add the ancho paste and return the browned chicken to the skillet. Continue to simmer, uncovered, until the chicken is tender and the liquid has reduced to a thick sauce, about 40 minutes.

Stir in 2 tablespoons of the chopped coriander. Add salt and pepper to taste.

To serve, divide the chicken equally onto 6 warmed plates. Pour the sauce evenly over chicken and sprinkle with the remaining tablespoon of coriander.

Cholesterol: 119 mg   Total Fat: 13 gm
Saturated Fat: 2 gm   Calories: 403

Yellow Squash and Corn Scramble

Here is a dish right out of a summer garden. In fact, as necessity is the mother of invention, we invented this dish to display the bounty of a proud client's harvest. The mellow yellows provide a felicitous contrast on the plate to the ancho chicken's vibrant reds. And the sweetness of the corn offsets the fire of the chilies. Feel free to substitute vegetables from your own crop, whether homegrown or purchased from your local market. Zucchini, eggplant, green tomatoes, and sweet peppers all work well and can help diminish a supply that threatens never to quit.

    3 medium ears corn, shucked, silk removed
    2 tablespoons extra-virgin olive oil
    3 medium yellow squash, cut lengthwise into quarters, then crosswise into
        ¼-inch slices
    2 tablespoons chopped fresh chives
    2 tablespoons chopped fresh parsley
    Salt
    Freshly ground black pepper

In a large pot combine the three ears of corn with just enough water to cover. Over high heat, bring to a boil. Drain immediately. When the corn is cool enough to handle, cut kernels from the cobs. Discard cobs.

Heat oil in a large nonstick frying pan (about 11-inch diameter) over medium heat. Add squash and corn. Cook, stirring occasionally, until squash is just tender but still has some crunch, about 8 minutes.

Add the chives and parsley. Stir to combine. Add salt and pepper to taste. Serve hot.

Cholesterol: 0 mg   Total Fat: 4 gm
Saturated Fat: 1 gm   Calories: 103

Angel Biscuits

These little angels are simply heaven. In contrast to the traditional ones, these yeast-risen biscuits are made without whole milk and with relatively little fat. A hint of sweetness makes them a natural foil for a devilish sauce like that of the chicken stew. Make extra dough. It can be refrigerated and made up in the morning for a celestial breakfast of warm biscuits and jam. Have any biscuits left? Try them in a summer berry shortcake.

$\frac{1}{2}$ cup evaporated skim milk
$1\frac{1}{2}$ teaspoons active dry yeast
4 teaspoons granulated sugar
$2\frac{1}{2}$ cups all-purpose flour
$\frac{1}{2}$ teaspoon baking powder
$\frac{1}{2}$ teaspoon baking soda
$\frac{1}{2}$ teaspoon salt
6 tablespoons solid vegetable shortening
$\frac{1}{2}$ cup low-fat buttermilk, at room temperature

In a small saucepan (2-cup capacity) heat the evaporated skim milk over medium heat until lukewarm (between 100 and 115 degrees). Pour milk into a small bowl.

Add the yeast and 1 teaspoon sugar. Stir to dissolve yeast. Set aside until liquid begins to foam, about 10 minutes.

Meanwhile, combine the remaining 3 teaspoons sugar with the flour, baking powder, baking soda, and salt in a large bowl. Stir with a whisk to combine. Sift into another large bowl.

Add the vegetable shortening and work it into the dry ingredients, using

197

your fingertips. The shortening will be properly incorporated when the mixture attains the consistency of coarse cornmeal.

Make a well in the center of the flour mixture. Add the buttermilk and the yeast mixture. Stir the liquid ingredients together and slowly incorporate the dry ingredients until a smooth ball of dough is formed.

Turn out onto a lightly floured work surface and pat into a 7½-inch square. Cut the dough into nine 2½-inch squares and place them on a foil-lined sheet pan ½ inch apart. Cover with a dry kitchen towel. Set aside in a warm, draft-free place for 30 minutes.

Preheat oven to 375 degrees.

Uncover the dough and place sheet pan in the center of the preheated oven. Bake until biscuits are well browned on top and bottom, about 15 minutes. Remove from oven and serve hot.

Yield: 9 biscuits

1 biscuit
Cholesterol: 1 mg   Total Fat: 8 gm
Saturated Fat: 2 gm   Calories: 219

Grapefruit, Jicama, and Endive Salad

We needed a salad for this meal that would be refreshing after all that spicy food. We put together all the adjectives we'd like in such a salad, and came up with ingredients to match. We wanted cool, we wanted crunchy, we wanted sweet, we wanted tangy. And we got just what we wanted.

2 ruby or pink grapefruit
½ pound jicama
1 pound Belgian endive
¼ cup Lime-Coriander Dressing (see below)

Cut the skin and pith away from the outside of the grapefruit. Section the fruit away from its inner membranes.

Peel the jicama. Cut it into batons ¼ inch square and 2 inches long.

Cut the endive leaves away from the bulbs. Wash and dry them.

To serve, toss the endive leaves with 2 tablespoons of dressing in a large bowl. Fan the leaves, cups upward and pointed ends outward, onto 6 chilled salad plates. In the same bowl, toss the grapefruit sections with 1 tablespoon of dressing. Cover the base ends of the endive spears with a loose mound of grapefruit. Toss the jicama with 1 tablespoon of dressing in the same bowl. Cascade the jicama batons over the grapefruit.

Cholesterol: 0 mg   Total Fat: 6 gm
Saturated Fat: 0 gm   Calories: 119

LIME-CORIANDER DRESSING

Grated rind of 1 lime
1 tablespoon freshly squeezed lime juice, strained
3 tablespoons white vinegar
1 teaspoon dry mustard
$1/4$ teaspoon ground coriander
$1/4$ teaspoon salt
$1/4$ teaspoon freshly ground pepper
$1/2$ cup extra-virgin olive oil
1 tablespoon finely chopped fresh coriander (cilantro)

In a small bowl, combine the lime peel and juice, vinegar, mustard, ground coriander, salt, and pepper. Stir with a whisk until well blended. Add the oil in a slow, thin stream while continuously whisking. When the oil is incorporated, stir in the fresh coriander.

Yield: $3/4$ cup

1 tablespoon
Cholesterol: 0 mg   Total Fat: 9 gm
Saturated Fat: 1 gm   Calories: 80

Bananas Baked in Phyllo with Caramel Sauce

Bananas cover all the bases of what's in these days. They're inexpensive, homey, and one of those comfort foods that are chock full of nostalgia. They make a perfect dessert food, since they taste the way people like their desserts, rich and sinful. High in potassium, they're also good for you. In this recipe they're all dressed up in phyllo dough and ready to go to the party.

$^1/_4$ cup granulated sugar
1 teaspoon ground cinnamon
6 medium bananas, very ripe but not mushy
1 large egg white, slightly beaten
Two 12 x 17-inch sheets of phyllo dough
Canola (or other vegetable) oil to brush pastry
1$^1/_4$ cups Caramel Sauce (see below)
Confectioners' sugar (optional)

Preheat oven to 350 degrees.

Combine sugar and cinnamon in a small bowl. Mix well. Transfer to a flat dish. Set aside.

One at a time, peel the bananas, brush with beaten egg white, and roll in cinnamon sugar. Make sure the entire surface of each banana is coated. Place bananas on a tray and set aside.

Lay a sheet of phyllo dough on a clean, dry work surface. Brush lightly with oil. Lay the other sheet of dough directly on top and brush it lightly with oil. Cut the phyllo lengthwise into 6 even strips, about 2 inches wide.

Wrap one strip of phyllo around each banana. Start at one end of the fruit and wind the pastry around it, slightly overlapping itself. Stop when you reach the opposite end. Trim off any excess dough. Lightly brush all sides of wrapped banana with more oil.

Place phyllo-wrapped bananas on a foil-lined baking sheet. Place pan in the center of the oven and bake until top of pastry is lightly browned, about 8 minutes. Turn each fruit and continue to bake until the other side is also lightly browned, about 8 more minutes. The pastry should be crisp and the banana soft when pierced with a toothpick.

To serve, remove the bananas from the oven. Place one in the center of each of 6 dessert plates. Pour the hot Caramel Sauce in a zigzag pattern over the top of the fruit, overlapping onto the plate. (The pattern of the sauce should cover the fruit and remain inside the border of the plate.)

Confectioners' sugar may be sifted over the whole plate to create a "snowy" effect. Serve hot.

Before adding sauce
Cholesterol: 0 mg   Total Fat: 5 gm
Saturated Fat: 1 gm   Calories: 225

CARAMEL SAUCE

1 cup granulated sugar
1/2 cup water
1/2 cup low-fat vanilla yogurt
1/2 teaspoon cinnamon

Combine sugar and water in a small saucepan (4-cup capacity). Heat over high heat, stirring constantly, until mixture comes to a boil. Stop stirring and allow mixture to boil until it becomes a dark amber color, 7–8 minutes.

Lower heat to medium and add yogurt, stirring constantly. (The mixture will quickly bubble up, then return to a normal boil.) Add cinnamon and continue to stir while mixture boils, until it becomes a smooth syrup, about 2 minutes. Remove it from heat. Cool slightly before serving.

Yield: About 1 1/4 cups

Note: The sauce can be made up to 1 week in advance and stored in an airtight container in the refrigerator. Before serving it, return it to a boil.

1 tablespoon
Cholesterol: 1 mg   Total Fat: 0
Saturated Fat: 0 gm   Calories: 41

Midsummer Night's Dream Dinner

Serves 6

Beet Risotto
Halibut with Red and Yellow Pepper Sauces
Raspberry Meringue Torte

Beet Risotto

My husband, a gifted and innovative chef, came up with this very good idea —
a gorgeous risotto (a dish that everybody adores) made without butter, cheese,
stock, or stirring. Its stunning ruby red color and exquisite taste make it a
perfect first course for the elegant dinner to follow.

6 tablespoons extra-virgin olive oil
3 medium shallots, peeled and finely chopped
1½ cups Arborio rice
1 cup dry white wine
3 cups beet juice (Biotta brand, available in health food stores)
Salt
Freshly ground black pepper
Freshly grated nutmeg
3 small garlic cloves, peeled and halved
1 pound beet greens, stalks removed, washed
½ cup toasted pine nuts

Preheat oven to 375 degrees.

Heat 3 tablespoons olive oil in a large, ovenproof pan over medium flame.
Add shallots and sauté until transparent, 4–5 minutes. Add rice and stir to coat
rice with oil and heat through, 2 minutes.

Add wine and beet juice and season lightly with salt, pepper, and nutmeg.
Bring to a boil.

Cover pan tightly with lid or aluminum foil and put in oven. Bake until the
rice is slightly chewy and of a creamy consistency, 20–25 minutes.

A few minutes before risotto is ready, heat remaining 3 tablespoons of oil in a
large sauté pan over medium flame. Add garlic and cook until lightly browned,
about 5 minutes. Remove garlic and discard. Add beet greens and cook until
wilted, 3–4 minutes. Season with salt and pepper to taste.

Remove risotto from oven. Taste for seasoning.

To serve, evenly distribute the beet greens over 6 warm plates. Mound a
portion of risotto on top of each bed of greens. Garnish with pine nuts.

Cholesterol: 0 mg   Total Fat: 17 gm
Saturated Fat: 3 gm   Calories: 341

Halibut with Red and Yellow Pepper Sauces

There was a period in our catering history when it seemed that a plate could not leave the kitchen with only one sauce. Everyone was delighted with the visual appeal of these multicolored menus, and the following dish was one of the most popular. A perfect summer entrée, it uses peppers just when they are at their most glorious, and most reasonably priced. The grilled halibut we've chosen here works beautifully, but so would any other firm, fresh, white-fleshed fish.

For the sauces:

3 large sweet red peppers, cored, seeded, and cut in pieces
6 medium shallots, peeled and coarsely chopped
6 tablespoons white wine
1½ cups Fish Stock (see page 236)
3 teaspoons dry sherry
Salt
Cayenne pepper
3 large sweet yellow peppers, cored, seeded, and cut in pieces

For the halibut:

6 halibut steaks, 6–7 ounces each
Extra-virgin olive oil
Salt
Freshly ground black pepper

Put red peppers, half the shallots, 3 tablespoons wine, and ¾ cup Fish Stock in a medium saucepan (about 2-quart capacity). Heat over medium flame and simmer until soft, 20–30 minutes.

Puree in a food processor. Strain through a sieve. Return to the saucepan and simmer over medium heat to the consistency of thick cream, about 10 minutes.

Add 1½ teaspoons sherry and season to taste with salt and cayenne pepper. Cover saucepan with lid and keep warm until ready to serve.

Repeat with yellow peppers and the remaining shallots, 3 tablespoons wine, ¾ cup Fish Stock, and 1½ teaspoons sherry. Season to taste with salt and cayenne pepper. Cover and keep warm.

Preheat oven to 300 degrees.

Preheat a ridged, nonstick grill pan over medium-high flame.

Rub the fish with a few drops of olive oil, salt, and pepper. Place as many steaks as will fit comfortably in the grill pan and cook over high heat until cross-hatch marks appear on fish, 3–4 minutes a side. Remove fish to a sheet pan lined with aluminum foil.

Continue in this manner until all the halibut steaks are grilled.

Place sheet pan in the preheated oven. Cook until fish is tender and flakes easily, 5–8 minutes.

Meanwhile, make a circular pool of the two pepper sauces on each of 6 dinner plates. Use the red pepper sauce to shape half the pool, the yellow pepper sauce for the other half.

To serve, place a cooked fish steak in the center of each plate, on the pool of sauces.

Note: The pepper sauces can be made a day ahead and stored in the refrigerator. Heat thoroughly before serving.

Cholesterol: 59 mg   Total Fat: 6 gm
Saturated Fat: 1 gm   Calories: 250

Raspberry Meringue Torte

Yes, we call this dramatic dessert a torte, but no, it isn't. It is not made with eggs; and its richness comes from flavor instead of fat. Bring this beauty to the table and watch the faces light up. Allow your guests to taste this sumptuous combination of gossamer filling, crunchy shell, and berry-rich topping. Now try to convince them they haven't been cheating on their cholesterol counts.

For the almond meringue shell:

1/2 cup ground toasted almonds

1 1/2 tablespoons cornstarch

2/3 cup granulated sugar

1/4 teaspoon salt

1/8 teaspoon cream of tartar

3 large egg whites, at room temperature

For the raspberry meringue filling:

¹/₂ cup granulated sugar

2 large egg whites, at room temperature

Pinch of cream of tartar

10 ounces frozen raspberries with syrup, thawed

1¹/₂ teaspoons powdered gelatin

3 tablespoons framboise or kirschwasser

For the topping:

1 pint fresh raspberries

1 tablespoon framboise or kirschwasser

1 tablespoon granulated sugar

Mint leaves

To make almond meringue shell, preheat oven to 200 degrees.

Line a baking sheet with parchment paper on which you have drawn a 9-inch circle.

Combine ground almonds, cornstarch, and ¹/₃ cup sugar. Set aside.

Add salt and cream of tartar to egg whites, and beat until soft peaks form. Slowly sprinkle in remaining sugar, and continue beating until stiff.

Using a rubber spatula, gently fold nut mixture into egg whites.

Fit a pastry bag with a large plain (or star) tip and fill it with the nut meringue. Pipe meringue onto parchment paper in touching concentric circles, starting at outer edge of drawn circle. Then pipe two more circles, one on top of the other, on top of outermost circle to form sides. Bake in oven until evenly dry and crisp, about 2¹/₂ hours.

Remove from oven and let cool for 15 minutes, then invert meringue and peel off paper. Set aside in an airtight container.

To make raspberry-meringue filling, combine all but 1 tablespoon sugar with 3 tablespoons water in a very small saucepan over medium heat. Stir until sugar dissolves, then lower heat and stop stirring. Continue to cook over low heat until syrup registers 248 degrees Fahrenheit (firm ball stage) on a candy thermometer.

While syrup cooks, using an electric beater, beat egg whites with a pinch of cream of tartar. When soft peaks begin to form, add remaining sugar and beat until stiff. (If sugar syrup has not reached 248 degrees at this point, raise heat to bring it up to temperature.)

While beating egg whites at medium speed, pour in sugar syrup in a thin stream, and continue to beat until cool, 2–3 minutes. (At this point the filling meringue can be stored, tightly covered, for about 2 hours at room temperature, 2 days in refrigerator, or a week in freezer.)

Puree raspberries in a food processor, then pass through a fine sieve to remove seeds. Set aside.

Combine gelatin and liqueur and let stand for 5 minutes. Put in top of double boiler and heat until gelatin dissolves, about 5 minutes. When dissolved, stir into raspberry puree. Refrigerate, stirring once or twice, until mixture begins to set, about 30 minutes. Remove from refrigerator and fold in meringue. Spoon raspberry-meringue filling into meringue shell, and refrigerate until set, about 30 minutes more.

To make topping, toss fruit, liqueur, and sugar together until fruit is moist and shiny. Just before serving, remove filled meringue shell from refrigerator, and pile berries on top of filling. Garnish with mint leaves.

Cholesterol: 0 mg   Total Fat: 6 gm
Saturated Fat: 1 gm   Calories: 281

Special-Occasion Buffet

Serves 12

Poached Salmon

Green Sauce

Potato Salad with Smoked Salmon Slivers

Cucumbers in Dill Sauce

Beefsteak Tomatoes with Basil

Roasted Garlic Cheese

Bread Basket

Summer Berries in Champagne

Poached Salmon

Poached salmon has appeared on more special-occasion menus than any other dish in our repertory. This is not surprising, since salmon has everything going for it — it is a fish without the offending "fishiness," a source of protein that is low in fat, calories, and cholesterol, and a food of outstanding flavor. Everybody loves it. Should you not be equipped with a fish poacher, not to worry. A large roasting pan will do. And as a dividend to the cook, since the fish is best at room temperature, it's ready when you are.

1 large lemon, cut in half
1 large carrot, peeled and cut in large pieces
1 large onion, peeled and cut in quarters
1 celery rib, washed and cut in large pieces
1 tablespoon salt
6 crushed black peppercorns
4 cups dry white wine
10 cups cold water
One 7–8-pound whole salmon, gutted, scaled, and flank removed
1 seedless European-style cucumber

Put the lemon, carrot, onion, celery, salt, peppercorns, wine, and water in a fish poacher (or deep roasting pan large enough to hold the salmon). Bring liquid to a boil over high heat.

Reduce heat and add the salmon, making sure it is completely immersed in the liquid. Poach over low heat for approximately 30 minutes, making sure the liquid remains at a simmer and doesn't boil.

Remove salmon from liquid and allow to cool. Discard the liquid. Refrigerate salmon, covered with plastic wrap, for at least 12 hours before serving.

To prepare a cucumber garnish, use a lemon stripper and work lengthwise, removing peel from cucumber at evenly spaced intervals to create a striped effect. With a slicer or very sharp knife, cut cucumber into very thin slices.

Before transferring the fish to a serving tray, remove the skin from its top side. The skin peels away easily from just behind the head to just in front of the tail. Carefully invert the fish onto serving tray and remove skin from the remaining side. In addition, remove any surface fat and dorsal fin bones.

Clean the surface of the serving tray before garnishing the fish with cucumber slices. Beginning at the tail end, fashion overlapping vertical rows of cucumber slices to resemble scales. Cover the entire exposed side of the fish (excluding head and tail) in this manner.

Set out two very large serving spoons alongside the salmon to make it easy for guests to serve themselves.

5 ounces
Cholesterol: 56 mg   Total Fat: 6 gm
Saturated Fat: 1 gm   Calories: 149

Green Sauce

Poached salmon is always accompanied by a green sauce. The fresh herbs that give it its vibrant color and cool, clean taste provide a refreshing contrast to the fish. It is usually made with mayonnaise and/or crème fraîche, both full of unhealthy fat and cholesterol. Ours is made with our low-cholesterol Mayonnaise and yogurt, so help yourself to seconds.

9 tablespoons nonfat plain yogurt
2 cups Mayonnaise (see page 238)
8 large leaves fresh spinach, stems removed, washed and wilted in lightly
    salted boiling water
5 tablespoons finely chopped fresh herbs (such as parsley, chervil, and dill)
Freshly squeezed juice of ½ lemon, strained
Dry white wine
Salt
Cayenne pepper

In the workbowl of a food processor, combine yogurt, Mayonnaise, spinach, herbs, and lemon juice. Process until a sauce the consistency of sour cream forms. If it is too thick, thin with a bit of wine. Add salt and cayenne pepper to taste.

Yield: Approximately 3 cups

Note: Sauce can be prepared ahead and refrigerated for 1 or 2 days.

2 tablespoons
Cholesterol: 0 mg   Total Fat: 14 gm
Saturated Fat: 2 gm   Calories: 122

Potato Salad with Smoked Salmon Slivers

Years ago, Irene Sax, a fine friend and food journalist, called, full of excitement. "I just ate the most wonderful thing at lunch. It would be perfect for catering."

The dish in question was a salad of new potatoes, threaded with slivers of smoked salmon and dotted with red caviar. The caviar, a leading cholesterol culprit, had to go. But no great loss. The salad is still superb. Make it ahead, giving the ingredients a chance to blend. It will taste even better.

3 pounds small red potatoes, washed
1/4 cup red wine vinegar
3 tablespoons extra-virgin olive oil
1 tablespoon chopped fresh chives
1 tablespoon chopped fresh parsley
Salt
Freshly ground black pepper
6 ounces smoked salmon (not lox), sliced into thin strips

In a large pot, boil the potatoes in lightly salted water until tender, about 20 minutes. Remove them from water, and cut into 1-inch pieces. Place the pieces in a bowl and pour 2 tablespoons of the vinegar over the potatoes.

Before serving, combine the rest of the vinegar, the oil, and the herbs and toss with the potatoes to coat.

Season to taste with salt and pepper. Add smoked salmon and retoss.

Cholesterol: 3 mg   Total Fat: 4 gm
Saturated Fat: 1 gm   Calories: 152

Cucumbers in Dill Sauce

This cool and refreshing salad is a traditional accompaniment to poached salmon. I share my two cucumber tricks with you. Julie Sahni, Indian cook extraordinaire, taught me the first. Before peeling the cucumber, cut a small slice off one end and rub it against the cucumber, cut surface to cut surface. Within moments a white froth will appear along the perimeter. This process will eliminate any bitterness. Second, salting the cucumbers and weighting them after they are sliced allows them to rid themselves of their excess liquid. In this way, the dressing is not diluted.

7 cucumbers, each about 8 inches long
$\frac{1}{2}$ cup tarragon vinegar
1 teaspoon salt
1 tablespoon granulated sugar
2 medium shallots, peeled and minced
$\frac{1}{2}$ teaspoon freshly ground black pepper
4 tablespoons finely chopped fresh dill

Peel the cucumbers. Cut them in half lengthwise, and scoop out and discard the seeds. Using a slicer or very sharp knife, cut cucumbers into thin slices. Put the slices into a colander. Sprinkle with 2 tablespoons of the vinegar, the salt, and $1\frac{1}{2}$ teaspoons of the sugar. Let stand for about 30 minutes. Drain and set aside in a bowl.

Make a dressing by whisking together the remaining vinegar and sugar, and the shallots. Pour some of it over the drained cucumbers and toss to coat. Add the remainder of the dressing, the pepper, and 3 tablespoons of the dill. Toss together. Correct seasoning for salt, pepper, and sugar.

Refrigerate for 30 minutes.

Before serving, retoss and sprinkle with the remaining chopped dill.

Cholesterol: 0 mg   Total Fat: 0 gm
Saturated Fat: 0 gm   Calories: 12

Beefsteak Tomatoes with Basil

When two of nature's greatest gifts team up, the result has got to be heaven. This divine dish is a feast for the eyes as well as the tastebuds. Giant beefsteak tomatoes are what we prefer, alternating the slices with behemoth basil leaves. But the tomatoes must be first-rate. Go to your most reliable source (for us, our local greenmarket, where they come fresh from the farm) and taste before you buy.

4 giant red beefsteak tomatoes, washed and dried
4 giant yellow beefsteak tomatoes, washed and dried
1 bunch basil, gently and thoroughly washed and dried

Using a serrated knife, slice tomatoes into 1/4-inch rounds.

On an attractive serving platter large enough to accommodate all the slices, alternate pieces of red and yellow tomato, inserting a large basil leaf after each slice.

Cholesterol: 0 mg   Total Fat: 0 gm
Saturated Fat: 0 gm   Calories: 33

Roasted Garlic Cheese

In the old days, we used to include a groaning board of cheeses on this buffet. We've replaced all that fat with this savory substitute. Surround it with water biscuits and watch it disappear. Roasting the garlic this way sweetens its flavor and softens the aftertaste. We also use this garlic squeezed onto croutons, stuffed under poultry skin, and slathered onto pasta. Keep some extra on hand; you'll come up with some uses of your own.

1 small head garlic
1 teaspoon canola (or other vegetable) oil

1 cup Yogurt Cheese (see page 239)
¹/₄ teaspoon salt
1 teaspoon finely chopped fresh parsley

Preheat oven to 475 degrees.

Slice top off the head of garlic. (The tops of all the garlic cloves should be exposed.) Drizzle oil over the top surface. Wrap the head of garlic in aluminum foil. Place it in a small baking dish and put it in the center of the preheated oven. Roast until the entire head of garlic is very tender and fragrant, about 1 hour. Remove from oven and allow to cool in the foil.

Remove the foil. Squeeze the garlic head to extract all the roasted garlic paste. Discard the shell.

In a small bowl, use a rubber spatula to thoroughly blend the yogurt cheese with 1 tablespoon of the roasted garlic paste and the salt.

Loosely line 2 half-cup molds (dry measuring cups work well) with plastic wrap so that it aprons over the edges. Densely pack each mold with the flavored cheese.

To serve, invert each mold onto the center of a serving plate. Lift off the molds and gently peel away the plastic wrap. Garnish the surface of the molded cheese with chopped parsley. Surround with crackers.

Yield: About 1 cup

1 tablespoon
Cholesterol: 1 mg   Total Fat: 0
Saturated Fat: 0 gm   Calories: 19

Bread Basket

While you are welcome to bake some of the breads located on other pages of this book for this buffet, you don't have to. Simply go to one or a number of local haunts whose breads you enjoy, and pick a variety of breads and rolls. Since presentation counts, keep color, size, and shape in mind when you make your choices, and arrange them in beautiful bowls, on boards, or in baskets.

Summer Berries in Champagne

The berries of the season are among summer's most wonderful gifts. To end this elegant buffet we pile them high in a huge glass bowl, bathe them in champagne with a splash of cassis, and garnish with fresh mint. What could be simpler, or more sublime?

½ cup brut champagne
1 tablespoon crème de cassis
2 teaspoons granulated sugar
2 pints strawberries, hulled and quartered
2 pints raspberries
2 pints blackberries
Fresh mint leaves for garnish

In a large bowl combine champagne, cassis, and sugar. Stir to dissolve sugar.

Add the strawberries, raspberries, and blackberries. Gently toss to coat fruit with the liquid. Refrigerate for at least 30 minutes before serving.

To serve, retoss fruit and liquid. Place in an attractive glass serving bowl and garnish with mint leaves.

Cholesterol: 0 mg   Total Fat: 1 gm
Saturated Fat: 0 gm   Calories: 78

Festive Finger Food for a Crowd

Serves 25

Tomato and Herbed Garlic Bruschette
Peanut and Garlic Chicken Sates
Chilled Mussels with Oregano Salsa
Turkey Burritos with Onion Relish
Smoked Salmon and Chive Cheese Triangles
Cherry Tomatoes with Peperonata
Sautéed Shrimp
Mushrooms in Bread Baskets
Charred Tuna on Daikon Wafers

Tomato and Herbed Garlic Bruschette

Bruschetta is Italy's garlic bread. The name is derived from a verb meaning "to roast over coals," the original way the bread was toasted. It began as poor people's fare, a way of extending the paltry menu, and crossed over to its current chic. These savory bread rounds can be dressed up any number of ways, two of which we offer here. Arrange them attractively on platters and conveniently locate them where your guests can help themselves.

BRUSCHETTA WITH FRESH TOMATO

1 long loaf cholesterol-free Italian bread
Extra-virgin olive oil
1 large garlic clove, peeled
1 pound ripe plum tomatoes, peeled and seeded
2 tablespoons balsamic vinegar
Salt
Freshly ground black pepper
6 large basil leaves, washed, dried, and cut into shreds

Preheat oven to 350 degrees.

Slice bread into ¹/₂-inch thick slices. Lightly brush one side of each slice with olive oil. Cut the garlic clove in half. Squeeze it slightly to express its juice. Rub the cut surface over the oiled surface of each piece of bread.

Bake bread slices, garlic side up, on a rack in the preheated oven until they have toasted light brown, 4–5 minutes.

Chop tomatoes into ¹/₄-inch dice. Dress with vinegar and a bit of olive oil. Season to taste with salt and pepper.

Top each piece of toast with about 1 tablespoon of the tomato mixture. Garnish with a few strands of basil.

1 slice
Cholesterol: 0 mg   Total Fat: 4 gm
Saturated Fat: 0.6 gm   Calories: 120

HERBED GARLIC BRUSCHETTA

2 long loaves cholesterol-free Italian bread (whole wheat or semolina
  bread may be substituted)
1/4 cup extra-virgin olive oil
1 large garlic clove, peeled and minced
1 tablespoon finely chopped fresh oregano leaves
2 tablespoons finely chopped fresh parsley
2 teaspoons whole-grain mustard
1/8 teaspoon salt
1/4 teaspoon freshly ground black pepper

Preheat oven to 350 degrees.

Slice each loaf of bread into 1/2-inch rounds.

In a small bowl, mix olive oil with garlic, oregano, parsley, mustard, salt, and pepper. Brush one side of each slice of bread with the mixture.

Bake slices on a rack, seasoned side up, in the preheated oven until the edges of the bread have browned, 6–8 minutes.

Serve warm or at room temperature.

Note: Unused herb mixture can be stored for a week in the refrigerator.

> *1 slice*
> Cholesterol: 0 mg   Total Fat: 2 gm
> Saturated Fat: 0.3 gm   Calories: 100

Peanut and Garlic Chicken Sates

Many people make a meal out of party hors d'oeuvres, so we always include at least one substantial protein choice like these. Served on skewers, these Indonesian tidbits are attractive and easy to handle. Made of skinned chicken breast, they are also light and low in fat. The perky peanut sauce is typical of the Indonesian dish and hard to resist. Provide plenty of napkins.

1/4 cup smooth peanut butter
1/4 cup canola (or other vegetable) oil

¼ cup soy sauce
Freshly squeezed juice of 1 lime
2 tablespoons chopped peeled fresh ginger
1 medium garlic clove, peeled and chopped
1 teaspoon ground coriander
Generous pinch cayenne pepper
13 chicken breast cutlets (skin removed), about 6 ounces each
½ cup finely chopped roasted peanuts

In the workbowl of a food processor or blender, puree the peanut butter, oil, soy sauce, lime juice, ginger, garlic, coriander, and cayenne pepper.

Slice each chicken cutlet lengthwise into 4 strips. Marinate the chicken in the puree for at least 1 hour before cooking.

Lace each piece of chicken onto the pointed half of a wooden skewer. To prevent burning, make sure that the point is covered by the chicken and the exposed portion of each skewer is covered with aluminum foil.

Preheat an oven broiler or charcoal grill. Cook sates for about 2 minutes on each side. Remove from heat and roll the end of each sate in chopped peanuts.

Serve immediately.

2 skewers
Cholesterol: 53 mg   Total Fat: 5 gm
Saturated Fat: 1 gm   Calories: 151

Chilled Mussels with Oregano Salsa

This hors d'oeuvre, with its sweet, meaty mussels and salsa kick, is delicious, great-looking, and couldn't be easier to make. As if that weren't enough, it can be done completely in advance, down to arranging it on trays.

½ cup coarsely chopped onion
1 bay leaf
2 cups water
½ cup dry white wine
Pinch cayenne pepper

5 pounds mussels in their shells (preferably cultivated), cleaned and
    debearded
2 Anaheim chilies, stems and seeds removed
1 pound ripe tomatoes, skinned and seeded
2 medium scallions
1/2 teaspoon minced garlic
1 tablespoon fresh oregano leaves
2 tablespoons chopped fresh parsley
2 tablespoons freshly squeezed lime juice
Salt
Freshly ground black pepper

In a pot large enough to hold all the mussels, combine the onion, bay leaf, water, wine, and cayenne pepper. Bring to a boil over high heat. Add the mussels. Cover the pot and continue cooking just until the mussels open, about 5 minutes.

Drain. Discard vegetable solids and any unopened mussels. When mussels are cool enough to handle, remove meat from the shell and refrigerate.

Clean and set aside one half shell for each mussel. Refrigerate.

To make salsa, coarsely chop chilies, tomatoes, and scallions. Combine them with the garlic, oregano, parsley, and lime juice in the workbowl of a food processor or blender. Process to a minced salsa, being careful not to liquefy.

Transfer to a saucepan. Simmer for about 5 minutes. Allow to cool. Season to taste with salt and pepper. Refrigerate, covered, until ready to use.

To serve, place one mussel on each half shell. Top with just enough salsa to cover the mussel meat.

Cholesterol: 19 mg   Total Fat: 2 gm
Saturated Fat: 0 gm   Calories: 67

Turkey Burritos
with Onion Relish

Mexican food is gaining on Italian as America's favorite cuisine. This great hors d'oeuvres was inspired by something similar from Bob Posch, who made his dish with duck. We use turkey, which cuts the cholesterol while keeping the rich flavor. These burritos pack a lot in a bite with all of their contrasts — sweet and sour, soft and crunchy, cool and full of fire.

For the relish:

1 cup finely minced onion
1 carrot, peeled and grated
2 tablespoons tomato paste
2 tablespoons cider vinegar
1 tablespoon granulated sugar
2 tablespoons extra-virgin olive oil
1/4 teaspoon salt
1/4 teaspoon freshly ground black pepper
Pinch hot red pepper flakes

For the turkey:

2 tablespoons extra-virgin olive oil
1 large garlic clove, peeled and squeezed through a press
1 tablespoon freshly squeezed lime juice
1/4 teaspoon ground coriander
1/4 teaspoon salt
1/4 teaspoon freshly ground black pepper
4 medium turkey thighs, skinned, boned, and butterflied

For the assembly:

2 bunches arugula, stems removed, leaves washed and dried
25 small flour tortillas brought to room temperature

To make relish, in a saucepan combine onion, carrot, tomato paste, vinegar, sugar, olive oil, salt, pepper, and red pepper flakes. Bring to a boil over high heat. Reduce heat. Cover pan and simmer for 30 minutes. At this point, if the consistency is too watery (it should be about like pickle relish), continue to cook uncovered until excessive liquid evaporates. Cool and refrigerate.

To prepare the turkey, make a marinade by combining the olive oil, garlic, lime juice, coriander, salt, and pepper in a small bowl. Brush each turkey thigh all over with this mixture. Refrigerate covered for at least 1 hour.

Preheat oven broiler or charcoal grill.

Broil or grill the turkey thighs (use a rack if you use the broiler) just until they are no longer pink in the center, 4–5 minutes a side. Cool. Carve into very thin slices.

To assemble the burritos, cut the tortillas in half. Place an arugula leaf perpendicular to the midpoint of the straight edge of each tortilla half, extending it slightly over the curved edge. Lay two or three slices of turkey lengthwise on the arugula. Spoon a scant teaspoon of onion relish on top of the turkey. Wrap the tortilla around its filling to form a cone. Secure in place with a round wooden toothpick.

Note: Relish can be made several days in advance and held in refrigerator in an airtight container.

> *2 burritos*
> Cholesterol: 37 mg   Total Fat: 4 gm
> Saturated Fat: 1 gm   Calories: 148

Smoked Salmon and Chive Cheese Triangles

This is classic finger food. We've been serving it since our first cocktail party, and people still take two at a time. We used to spread the bread with butter, but this healthier chive cheese is even better. We warn you, once the guests arrive, these little triangles will fly off the trays, so make up plenty in advance.

1 cup Yogurt Cheese (see page 239)
1 tablespoon very finely chopped fresh chives
1/2 teaspoon freshly ground black pepper
13 slices thin-sliced whole-grain bread
1 pound finely sliced smoked salmon (not lox), trimmed of its dark flesh
4–6 stems fresh dill, cleaned and dried

In a small bowl, thoroughly combine the Yogurt Cheese, chives, and pepper. Cover one side of each slice of bread with a uniform smear of the flavored cheese.

Lay a single layer of salmon on top of the cheese. Position the salmon so there are no gaps. The fish should hang slightly over the crust.

Using a sharp knife, cut down through the salmon just inside the crust to trim the sandwich square. Cut each square into four triangles.

Pluck ³/₄-inch dill sprigs from their stems. Garnish each triangle with one dill sprig.

2 triangles
Cholesterol: 4 mg   Total Fat: 1 gm
Saturated Fat: 0 gm   Calories: 52

Cherry Tomatoes with Peperonata

The bite size and visual appeal of the cherry tomato make it a natural when it comes to hors d'oeuvres. Before we got wise to cholesterol, we would fill these little guys with mayonnaisy salads or butter-based spreads. Now we use this Italian pepper mix, and they go even faster.

50 large cherry tomatoes (rather firm), washed
3 large, straight-sided sweet yellow peppers
3 large, straight-sided sweet red peppers
2 medium zucchini
1 large eggplant
5 tablespoons extra-virgin olive oil
2 medium shallots, peeled and chopped
2 medium garlic cloves, peeled and chopped
5 canned Italian plum tomatoes (preferably from San Marzano), cut in
    small pieces
¹/₂ teaspoon granulated sugar
1 teaspoon tomato paste
Pinch hot red pepper flakes
Sprig fresh thyme

Sprig fresh rosemary
Salt
Pepper

Cut a small slice off the top of each cherry tomato. Set tops aside. Scoop out the insides of the tomatoes and discard, leaving the shells. Invert them on several thicknesses of paper towel to drain. Refrigerate.

To prepare peppers, cut a slice off the top and bottom of each. Cut the remainder in half vertically, creating two rectangular shapes for each pepper. Discard the seeds and membrane and remove skin using a sharp vegetable peeler. Using a very sharp knife, cut the flesh into tiny cubes. Reserve.

To prepare zucchini, cut off the skin in long strips, leaving about $1/4$-inch flesh attached to skin. Discard the rest of the zucchini, or use in another recipe. Dice the strips into tiny cubes.

To prepare eggplant, follow the procedure for zucchini.

Heat 1 tablespoon of the oil in a nonstick frying pan and add pepper cubes. Sauté over medium heat until tender but still somewhat firm, 2–3 minutes. Remove pepper pieces and set aside.

Using the same pan, repeat this method for zucchini and eggplant, adding 1 tablespoon olive oil each time. Remove the zucchini and eggplant from the pan and reserve.

Heat the remaining 2 tablespoons of oil in the same pan and sauté shallots and garlic over low heat until soft, 2–3 minutes.

Add the tomatoes, sugar, tomato paste, pepper flakes, thyme, and rosemary and cook until a thick mixture is achieved, about 10 minutes. Puree it in the workbowl of a food processor and strain through a sieve into a bowl. Add the reserved vegetable cubes and salt and pepper to taste. Remove to an ovenproof pot.

Preheat oven to 400 degrees.

Cover pot and heat in oven for 20 minutes. Remove and allow to cool.

To serve, fill the reserved tomato shells with peperonata and place a tomato top, at an angle, on each one.

Note: Peperonata mixture can be prepared in advance and refrigerated, covered tightly, for up to 2 days.

2 tomatoes
Cholesterol: 0 mg   Total Fat: 3 gm
Saturated Fat: 0 gm   Calories: 48

Sautéed Shrimp

These savory shellfish are so popular that guests line up outside the kitchen waiting for them to be served. They are a cinch to prepare and easy to cook. But be prepared to be in the kitchen, since they must be made at the last minute. Provide plenty of them, the bigger the better, and watch them disappear.

3 tablespoons extra-virgin olive oil
4 medium shallots, peeled and finely chopped
75 large shrimp, peeled and deveined
6 tablespoons dry white wine
1 tablespoon finely chopped fresh parsley
2 teaspoons finely chopped fresh dill
Salt
Freshly ground black pepper
Freshly squeezed lemon juice
1 lemon half

In a large nonstick frying pan heat the olive oil over medium heat. Reduce heat to low and sauté the shallots for several minutes, making sure they do not brown.

Add shrimp (25 at a time). Turn heat up slightly and add one-third of the wine and herbs. Cook shrimp on both sides for about 2 minutes. Add salt, pepper, and lemon juice to taste. Put a toothpick in each shrimp and serve hot.

Repeat with subsequent batches of shrimp, keeping the shallots that you have already used in the pan and adding wine and herbs.

Note: Place a lemon half, cut side up, on the serving tray (cut a slice off its bottom so that it will sit by itself). Guests can insert their used toothpicks in it.

3 shrimp
Cholesterol: 130 mg   Total Fat: 4 gm
Saturated Fat: 1 gm   Calories: 108

Mushrooms in Bread Baskets

Our hors d'oeuvre repertoire is constantly changing, but a few old standards put in regular appearances. This mélange of wild and domestic mushrooms heads the list. We used to prepare it with butter and cream. We've switched to fresh herbs and olive oil, a change that produces a heartier mushroom flavor and is better for your heart besides.

1 package very thin-sliced cholesterol-free white bread
2 ounces dried porcini mushrooms
2 pounds fresh shiitake mushrooms (other wild varieties may be combined
    or substituted), stems removed and discarded
2 tablespoons extra-virgin olive oil
2 medium shallots, peeled and finely chopped
1 tablespoon finely chopped fresh parsley
Salt
Freshly ground black pepper
1–2 tablespoons port wine
Freshly grated Parmesan cheese (optional)

Preheat oven to 350 degrees.

Using a 1³/₄ x 1³/₄-inch cutter, cut 50 squares from the bread. With your fingers, gently press each piece into the opening of a miniature muffin tin. Bake in the preheated oven until crisp and slightly brown, 8–10 minutes. Remove and allow to cool in the tin.

In warm water to cover, soak the porcini for several hours. Remove the mushrooms from the liquid and rinse thoroughly in running water to remove grit. Chop and set aside. Strain the soaking liquid through a paper coffee filter to remove grit and reserve.

Clean and chop the fresh mushrooms and set aside.

In a large nonstick frying pan heat olive oil and add shallots. Sauté over low heat until shallots are soft, about 2 minutes. Add all mushrooms and the soaking liquid and, raising the heat to medium, cook, stirring occasionally, for 15–20 minutes, or until all the liquid has evaporated.

Add parsley and salt and pepper to taste. Add port and cook several additional minutes until it evaporates. Remove mushrooms from heat.

To serve, fill each bread cup with the mushroom mixture. Dust with Parmesan cheese, if desired. Heat in a 350-degree oven for 10 minutes, and serve hot.

Note: Bread cups can be made in advance and kept overnight in an airtight container or frozen. Mushroom mixture can also be prepared ahead and kept under refrigeration for 2–3 days.

2 mushroom cups, without cheese
Cholesterol: 0 mg   Total Fat: 1 gm
Saturated Fat: 0 gm   Calories: 72

Charred Tuna on Daikon Wafers

This beautiful canapé takes its inspiration from the popular Japanese sashimi. We seduce the squeamish by giving the tuna a quick grilling and pair it with a circle of crunchy daikon, which makes it easier to handle.

3 pounds daikon (large white Japanese radish), cleaned and peeled
3 tablespoons wasabi powder (available in Oriental food shops)
2 pounds sushi-quality fresh loin of tuna
Soy sauce
2 tablespoons ground coriander
1 tablespoon salt
1 tablespoon freshly ground white pepper
3 medium scallions, green part only, washed and trimmed

Slice daikon crosswise into $\frac{1}{8}$-inch wafers. (If daikon is more than $1\frac{1}{2}$ inches in diameter, use a $1\frac{1}{2}$-inch pastry cutter to shape each wafer into a disk.) Cover with a damp paper towel and set aside.

Mix the wasabi powder with enough water to make a smooth paste. It should not be runny.

Cut tuna into slices 1 inch thick. Cut each slice into 1-inch wide strips. Lightly brush the entire surface of the fish with soy sauce.

In a small bowl, mix together the coriander, salt, and pepper. Using this mixture, coat the tuna, shaking off any excess.

In a very hot iron skillet, char each surface of the tuna. (The fish should be seared on the surface, but raw in the center.)

Slice pieces of tuna crosswise, very thinly.

Slice the scallion greens into very thin rings. Fan 2 slices of tuna on each daikon wafer. Using the tip of a paring knife, transfer a small bit of wasabi paste (about the size of a split pea) to the center of the topmost tuna slice. Distribute a few scallion rings over the wasabi.

Serve immediately.

Yield: 75 or more canapés

About 3 canapés
Cholesterol: 16 mg   Total Fat: less than 1 gm
Saturated Fat: less than 1 gm   Calories: 56

FOUNDATIONS

Stocks and Sauces

Beef Stock
Chicken Stock
Brown Chicken Stock
Fish Stock
Lobster Stock
Mayonnaise
Yogurt Cheese
Whipped Yogurt Cream
Raspberry Sauce

Beef Stock

4–5 pounds beef bones (with some meat on), broken into pieces
2 medium onions, peeled and coarsely chopped
1 large carrot, peeled and coarsely chopped
1 large celery rib, coarsely chopped
1 large garlic clove, peeled
2 ounces tomato paste
1 cup red wine
Approximately 3 quarts water
2 whole cloves

Preheat oven to 450 degrees.

Place beef bones on a sheet pan. Put pan in center of oven and roast bones until well browned, about 45 minutes.

Add the onions, carrot, celery, and garlic to the pan and smear the tomato paste on the bones. Continue to roast, 10–15 minutes longer. Remove pan from oven. Drain and discard fat.

Place contents of sheet pan into large stockpot (about 8-quart capacity), scraping pan to remove all browned particles. Add wine, water, and cloves. The bones should be covered with liquid. Bring to a boil. Reduce heat and simmer uncovered about 5 hours. As the stock simmers, periodically skim off debris that rises to the surface.

Strain stock, discarding solids, and cool liquid to room temperature. Place in a container and seal with an airtight lid. Refrigerate overnight. Remove fat that has risen to the surface. Return to refrigerator until ready to use.

Yield: About 2 quarts

Note: Stock will keep several days in refrigerator. It may be frozen for several months.

1 cup
Cholesterol: 5 mg   Total Fat: 1 gm
Saturated Fat: 0 gm   Calories: 32

Chicken Stock

3–4 pounds chicken bones, broken into pieces
1 large onion, peeled and coarsely chopped
1 leek, washed thoroughly and coarsely chopped
2–3 shallots, peeled and coarsely chopped
1 large carrot, peeled and coarsely chopped
1 large celery rib, coarsely chopped
3–4 sprigs parsley
3 quarts water

Combine all ingredients in a large stockpot (about 8-quart capacity) and bring to a boil over high heat. As soon as liquid begins to boil, reduce heat and simmer uncovered until reduced by a third, about 3 hours. As the stock simmers, periodically skim off debris that rises to the surface.

Strain the stock and discard solids. Cool the liquid to room temperature.

Place in a container and seal with an airtight lid. Refrigerate overnight. Remove fat that has risen to the surface. Return to refrigerator until ready to use.

Yield: About 2 quarts

Note: Stock will keep several days in refrigerator. It may be frozen for several months.

1 cup
Cholesterol: 1 mg   Total Fat: 2 gm
Saturated Fat: 0 gm   Calories: 45

Brown Chicken Stock

3–4 pounds chicken bones, broken into pieces
1 large onion, peeled and coarsely chopped
1 leek, washed thoroughly and coarsely chopped
2–3 large shallots, peeled and coarsely chopped
1 large carrot, peeled and coarsely chopped

1 large celery rib, coarsely chopped
1 large garlic clove, peeled
1½ ounces tomato paste
3 quarts water
3–4 sprigs fresh parsley

Preheat oven to 450 degrees.

Place bones on a sheet pan. Put pan in center of oven and roast bones until well browned, 30–40 minutes.

Add onion, leek, shallots, carrot, celery, and garlic to the pan and smear the tomato paste over the bones. Continue to roast until vegetables brown, 10–15 minutes longer. Remove pan from oven. Drain and discard fat.

Place contents of sheet pan into large stockpot (about 8-quart capacity), scraping sheet pan to remove all browned particles. Add water and parsley sprigs. Bring just to a boil over high heat. Immediately reduce to a simmer. Simmer uncovered until liquid reduces by one-third, about 3 hours. As stock simmers, periodically skim off debris that rises to the surface.

Strain stock, discarding solids, and cool liquid to room temperature.

Place in a container and seal with an airtight lid. Refrigerate overnight. Remove layer of fat that has risen to the surface. Return to refrigerator until ready to use.

Yield: About 2 quarts

Note: Stock will keep several days in refrigerator. It may be frozen for several months.

1 cup
Cholesterol: 1 mg   Total Fat: 2 gm
Saturated Fat: 0 gm   Calories: 56

Fish Stock

2 pounds fish bones (with heads if possible), from white fish, well rinsed
1 small carrot, peeled and coarsely chopped
1 small onion, peeled and coarsely chopped
1 celery rib, coarsely chopped

4 sprigs fresh parsley
1 bay leaf
6 black peppercorns
3 allspice berries
1 cup dry white vermouth
7 cups water

In a large stockpot (6–8-quart) combine all ingredients. Bring to a simmer over medium flame. (Do not allow to boil or stock will taste bitter.) Adjust heat to keep liquid at a simmer for 30 minutes. Skim any debris that rises to the surface.

Remove pot from heat. Strain liquid, discarding solids. Cool stock to room temperature. Refrigerate in an airtight container.

Yield: About 7 cups

Note: Stock may be kept for several days in refrigerator or frozen for several months.

1 cup
Cholesterol: 21 mg   Total Fat: 1 gm
Saturated Fat: 0 gm   Calories: 45

Lobster Stock

1–1½ pound lobster
2 tablespoons extra-virgin olive oil
1 small onion, peeled and coarsely chopped
1 small carrot, peeled and quartered
1 celery rib, cut in thirds
2 plum tomatoes, halved
1 leek, green top only, coarsely chopped
4 black peppercorns
1 bay leaf
3–4 sprigs fresh parsley
½ cup dry white vermouth
6 cups water

Using rubber gloves or covering lobster with a clean kitchen towel, twist tail and claws away from torso. (If you are squeamish about doing this to a live lobster, you can kill it first by cooking, covered, 2–3 minutes in 2–3 inches boiling water.) Crack claws and tail to extract the meat and coarsely chop it. Using a mallet or large knife, break up the claw and tail shells. Place lobster meat, body, and shells in a bowl and set aside.

Heat oil in 6-quart stockpot until very hot. Then add lobster meat, shells, and body. Stir over medium-high heat until shells turn bright red. Add remaining ingredients and allow to just begin to boil. Immediately reduce heat to just below a simmer. (Stock should only bubble occasionally.) Allow to reduce 1¹/₂ hours without stirring.

Remove from heat and pour stock through a sieve to separate liquid, which should then be passed through several layers of cheesecloth to extract any sediment. Discard lobster solids.

Cool stock to room temperature. Refrigerate in an airtight container.

Yield: Approximately 1 quart

Note: Stock will keep in refrigerator 4–5 days. It may also be frozen for several months.

1 cup
Cholesterol: 21 mg   Total Fat: 1 gm
Saturated Fat: 0 gm   Calories: 45

Mayonnaise

2 large egg whites, at room temperature
4 teaspoons Dijon-style mustard
2 tablespoons Japanese rice wine vinegar or plain vinegar
¹/₂ teaspoon salt
Freshly ground white pepper
1 cup canola (or other vegetable) oil
¹/₄ cup extra-virgin olive oil

In workbowl of a food processor combine the egg whites, mustard, vinegar, salt, and pepper. Then, with the machine running, slowly add the oils in a thin, steady stream. This will result in a creamy white mayonnaise. Taste and adjust salt and pepper.

(The mayonnaise can be made by hand. Use a whisk to combine ingredients and proceed as above. Be very careful not to add oils too quickly, or mixture will separate.)

Yield: 2 cups

Note: Refrigerate mayonnaise at least 1 hour before serving. Can be kept under refrigeration for 1 week.

1 tablespoon

Cholesterol: 0 mg	Total Fat: 8 gm
Saturated Fat: 2 gm	Calories: 77

Yogurt Cheese

8 ounces plain nonfat yogurt
Have on hand: cheesecloth and string

Make a 10-inch square of cheesecloth, 8 layers thick. Set aside.

Open container of yogurt. Pour off any excess liquid. Empty the contents of the container into the center of the cheesecloth square you have prepared. Gather corners of cloth together around yogurt and tie with string.

Tie the string to the midpoint of the handle of a long wooden spoon and suspend the ball of yogurt in cheesecloth over a bowl deep enough to allow the package to hang freely a couple of inches above the bottom of the bowl.

After 4–5 hours about ¹/₂ cup liquid will have drained from the yogurt. Discard this liquid.

Remove the package of yogurt from the spoon and untie the string. In the center of the cheesecloth will be a thick ball of Yogurt Cheese, similar in texture to a soft cream cheese.

Yield: ¹/₂ cup

Note: Yogurt Cheese may be stored for a week in an airtight container, under refrigeration.

1 tablespoon
Cholesterol: 1 mg   Total Fat: 0 gm
Saturated Fat: 0 gm   Calories: 16

Whipped Yogurt Cream

Show me a caterer, I'll show you cream — sweet cream, sour cream, whipped cream, double cream, light cream, heavy cream, crème fraîche, cream cheese, triple crème. How would we ever manage without it and still make people happy? What would we use to garnish our desserts and fancy up our breakfasts? Thank goodness we came up with Whipped Yogurt Cream. Five minutes' work produces a heavenly taste whose richness and flavor stand up to any high-fat alternative. Paired with a fruit sauce, this is even a great dessert all by itself.

²/₃ cup Yogurt Cheese (see preceding recipe)
1 tablespoon granulated sugar
¹/₂ teaspoon pure vanilla extract

Using a whisk, whip the Yogurt Cheese in a small bowl until thick and smooth, 2–3 minutes.

Add the sugar and vanilla extract and continue to whip 1 minute more. Cover bowl tightly with plastic wrap and refrigerate 1 hour before serving.

Yield: ²/₃ cup

Note: This topping will keep in refrigerator for several days.

1 tablespoon
Cholesterol: 1 mg   Total Fat: 0 gm
Saturated Fat: 0 gm   Calories: 20

Raspberry Sauce

One 10-ounce package frozen raspberries, thawed, with their juice
2 teaspoons freshly squeezed lemon juice, strained
1 tablespoon granulated sugar
2 tablespoons framboise or cassis

Combine all ingredients in the workbowl of a food processor. Puree. Pass through a fine strainer to remove seeds.

Yield: approximately 1¼ cups

Note: Sauce may be refrigerated in a covered container 4–5 days or kept frozen several months.

2 tablespoons
Cholesterol: 0 mg   Total Fat: 0 gm
Saturated Fat: 0 gm   Calories: 40

Index